COASTAL PATHS
OF THE SOUTH WEST

COASTAL PATHS OF THE SOUTH WEST

by

EDWARD C. PYATT

DAVID & CHARLES
NEWTON ABBOT

Set in 10 pt on 12 pt Times Roman
and printed in Great Britain
by Clarke Doble & Brendon Limited
for David & Charles (Publishers) Limited
South Devon House   Newton Abbot   Devon

CONTENTS

CONTENTS

LIST OF ILLUSTRATIONS

INTRODUCTION

THE National Parks and Access to the Countryside Act of 1949 was the culmination of a long series of attempts, going back more than half a century, to secure statutory recognition of our right to enjoy the wilder parts of England's countryside. For a time it seemed that a real advance had at last been made in the preservation of amenities and that we might look forward to continuing improvement in various outdoor issues, access, rights of way, and so forth, which had for so long seemed hopeless. The executive body set up under the Act, known as the National Parks Commission, was charged with the task of designating and developing certain areas as National Parks, and began its work with a will—the future seemed to be full of hope.

Now, more than twenty years later, we know that there are threats to the amenities of the countryside that have prevailed, not once but many times, against the spirit of the Act. We have seen hydro-electric schemes, industrial and water supply reservoirs, military training grounds and ranges, television and radio masts, radar installations, power lines and extensive afforestation in our National Parks, which we believed to have been preserved for us. Preserved they certainly are—for really intensive despoliation. Recently we have seen land bequeathed to the National Trust for preservation for all time and then taken over by legal act for development; we have seen motorways routed through Nature Reserves, atomic power stations strewn along flat coastlines. Indeed there would seem to be no defence against the spread of the technological age.

Peter Simple of the *Daily Telegraph* describes the situation in his characteristic way:

> 'We cannot,' says the Minister for Planning and Land, 'totally forbid reservoirs in national parks and areas of outstanding natural beauty, prohibit afforestation or the application of modern farming methods, the winning of raw materials and all other developments.'

It is becoming more and more obvious, in fact, that although

9

these developments are incompatible with the idea of national parks as it was first conceived by an earlier, more civilised tribe of planners, we cannot forbid them at all.

When greed of gain (whether disguised as 'inevitable progress', 'the national interest', 'higher living standards' or otherwise) fights with natural beauty, there is never any doubt which will be the winner.

There is only one conclusion to be drawn from the arguments of the Minister for Planning and Land or of other public apologists who claim to be able to do two opposite things at the same time. It is this. If you want to see what is left of our country, go and look at it quickly. It will not be there much longer.

Among the provisions of the 1949 Act was one for the setting up of certain long-distance footpaths. The work on these proved unexpectedly complex and took longer than was originally envisaged, but nevertheless a number are now available—the Pennine Way (250 miles from Derbyshire to the Scottish border), the Cleveland Way (93 miles over the North Yorks Moors, the Cleveland Hills and along the Yorkshire coast), and the Pembrokeshire Coast Path (167 miles from Amroth to St Dogmaels). Considerable progress has been made on the South Downs Way (80 miles from Beachy Head to the Hampshire border), Offa's Dyke Path (168 miles along the Welsh border), the North Downs Way (141 miles from Farnham to Dover), and the South-West Peninsula Coast Path (over 500 miles from Minehead to Studland). The last is the subject of this book.

Once again Peter Simple has drawn attention to possible dangers:

Mr Arthur Skeffington, joint Parliamentary Secretary Ministry of Housing, says that the Government, by the terms of the Countryside Act of 1968, is aiming to provide a thousand miles of new footpaths for the enjoyment of walkers.

These, like the Pennine Way, will be in attractive parts of the country and will supplement the 86,000 miles of footpaths and bridleways which are said to exist in England and Wales already.

Perhaps so. But it is also possible that these new, official, State-sponsored footpaths (or 'walkerways' as they might be called) will help to complete the process by which the old footpaths are being dug up, fenced off and otherwise obliterated from use and memory.

In a forward-looking country it is simply a nuisance for forward-looking people, such as scientific farmers or scientific forestry-managers, to have walkers wandering about unorganised all over the place and getting in the way of their scientific operations.

It would be much more convenient if these walkers could be channelled into designated routes, their numbers being controlled by computers. If they showed any tendency to stray, they could be firmly escorted back to the approved path by a new corps of Countryside Pedestrian Traffic Control Wardens.

It will of course never come to this; though when we compare the realisation of today with our hopes of 1949 concerning many aspects of the Act we may well ponder on what may happen if we do not remain eternally vigilant.

*   *   *

The five hundred miles of West Country coastline is divided here into twenty-two sections averaging between twenty and twenty-five miles each; for each section there is a sketch plan (to a scale of two miles to one inch), a general introduction followed by a route description, and a local bibliography. The plans are not of a

The Countryside Commission's waymarking sign

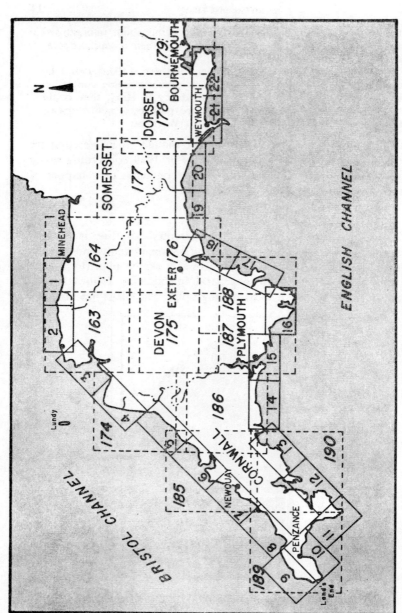

Key plan for sketch maps

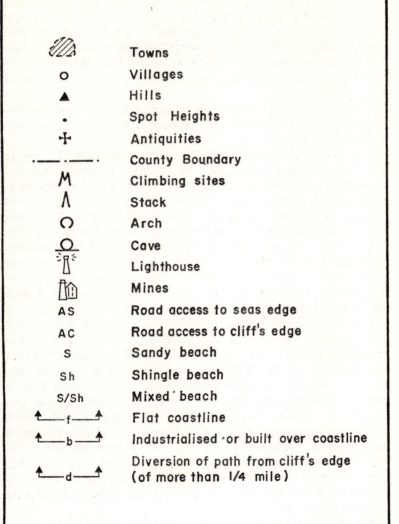

	Towns
o	Villages
▲	Hills
.	Spot Heights
⊹	Antiquities
——·——	County Boundary
M	Climbing sites
Λ	Stack
Ω	Arch
	Cave
	Lighthouse
	Mines
AS	Road access to seas edge
AC	Road access to cliff's edge
S	Sandy beach
Sh	Shingle beach
S/Sh	Mixed beach
↑—f—↑	Flat coastline
↑—b—↑	Industrialised or built over coastline
↑—d—↑	Diversion of path from cliff's edge (of more than 1/4 mile)

Symbols used on sketch maps

scale large enough to replace the One Inch Ordnance Survey Map which remains a must for the serious walker in the field. Route indications all refer to the eventual line of the Path; the physical state of paths existing at the time of writing is given in Appendix XI. In the end the Path will be waymarked by the acorn sign reproduced here and by finger boards bearing the legend 'Coastal Path'.

There are further appendices on topics likely to interest the traveller on the Path, each with bibliographies indicating a range of further reading.

The ideal way to travel the Path is to pass ever onwards, staying at a different place each night. The bountiful supply of bed and breakfast accommodation in the West Country makes this comparatively straightforward, and there is no need for advance booking, except perhaps in the school holiday season. The chain of youth hostels, if occasionally offering a somewhat lengthy day, can be similarly used, though booking may well be necessary. Many users of the Path will come by car and either make short round trips or return to the car by public transport at the end of the day. A party with two cars can arrange to leave one at each end of a projected walk.

The prospects of camping or bivouacking are not good. Camp sites are limited in number and frequently crowded, though it is probable that the Countryside Commission will do something about this problem once the Path is a going concern. The chief difficulty for the sleeper-out is water supply; as no natural water here is suitable, drinking water must be procured in advance (this means begging as there are but few public water supplies) and carried for use in bivouacs. Even when equipment is kept to a minimum the additional requirements for this sort of progress add quite seriously to the daily load-carrying. The bivouacker on the other hand is the only person free to enjoy the glories of the early morning, between 6.00 and 9.00 am, often the pleasantest and least crowded part of the day.

The traveller on the Path may become irked eventually by always having the sea on the same side; long periods of walking across a slope are said (and some will have us believe) to make one leg longer than the other. This fate can be avoided by the following ploy: Minehead to Barnstaple (train to Exeter); Exeter to Par (train to Newquay); Newquay to St Ives (train to Penzance); Penzance round Land's End to St Ives (train to Penzance); Penzance to Par (train to Newquay); Newquay to Barnstaple (train to Exeter); Exeter to Studland. Use of buses would multiply the possibilities many times.

I shall not recommend either a technique for walking or the equipment to go with it. Shoes need to be stout; two widely differing pairs changed about provide restful variety. Thorny vegetation calls for long trousers rather than shorts. It will rain, it will blow, the sun will shine brightly—appropriate counter-garments will be needed.

The Path follows the cliff edge as nearly as possible; where the beach provides a reasonable alternative this has been indicated in the text. Places where the Path is forced to diverge more than a quarter of a mile from the cliff edge are indicated on the sketch plans. The indentations of the coast often make the official route a long way round and, near the end of the day or when the weather is indifferent, we may find ourselves taking shorter cuts. As Harper wrote in one of his Cornish coast books: 'Very few are those who, exploring the rugged and greatly indented coasts of Cornwall, endure to the end and do not presently take some of the distant headlands and the obscure nooks and corners on trust.'

The sport has no rules except those of commonsense and consideration for others. Tremendous scope remains for enjoying all the good things this coastline has to offer.

THE COUNTRY CODE

Guard against all fire risk
Fasten all gates
Keep dogs under proper control
Keep to paths across farmland
Leave no litter
Safeguard water supplies
Protect wildlife, plants and trees
Go carefully on country roads
Respect the life of the countryside

SOME DON'TS FOR WALKERS ON THE PATH

Don't

—go near the cliff edge until you are sure that it is not crumbling or overhanging
—go near the cliff edge unless you are sure of yourself
—set out on a beach traverse on a rising tide
—embark on expeditions involving rock scrambling unless you have had climbing experience elsewhere

Page 17 Great Hangman to Foreland Point, North Devon (looking E). These are the great hog's back cliffs which rise to Great Hangman and Holdstone and Trentishoe Downs. The outjutting headlands are Foreland Point (far off), then Highveer Point with Blackstone Point near at hand

Page 18 Clovelly, North Devon (looking W). The village and its harbour at low tide. Beyond is the steep face of Gallantry Bower and the high cliff line running towards Hartland Point

1

MINEHEAD TO LYNTON

Minehead - Porlock - Foreland Point
Lynmouth - Lynton

THE whole of this magnificent stretch of coastline lies within the bounds of the Exmoor National Park. The National Trust has coastal properties in the neighbourhood of Bossington and Selworthy, while its Watersmeet Estate at Lynton lies just behind the coast. A range of hills running parallel to the sea rises to over a thousand feet for much of the way, broken only by a wide gap at Porlock and the steep narrow gorge of the East and West Lyn Rivers which join at Lynmouth. From Minehead to a point somewhat west of Foreland Point the rocks are Foreland Grits, predominantly sandstones; westwards to Lynton are the slatey rocks of the Lynton Beds. All are Lower Devonian.

By the Path, Minehead to Porlock is $7\frac{1}{2}$ miles, Porlock to County Gate $6\frac{1}{2}$ miles and County Gate to Lynmouth 6 miles—a total of 20.

MINEHEAD (SS96/9745/46). On A39. Nearest station—Taunton (24m).
Steamer service up and down the coast and across to Wales. Youth Hostel. National Park Information Centre. E.C. Weds.
The *Thorough Guide* (1903) says of it 'not so long ago an unsavoury village, has developed into a comely little seaside town'. Thus it remains today with its harbour and sands and large holiday camp. Divided into Lower Town—the main shopping centre, Quay Town (harbour and fishermen's cottages) and Upper Town on the slopes of North Hill, with steep streets and St Michael's Church, it is a good walking centre.

North Hill rises above Minehead, in the words of an ancient guide-book, 'extremely steep and rugged. The rocks hang at a prodigious height above the houses and seem every moment to threaten them with destruction.' The Path climbs up through Culver Cliff Wood. There are several alternative lines and soon there are views up

B

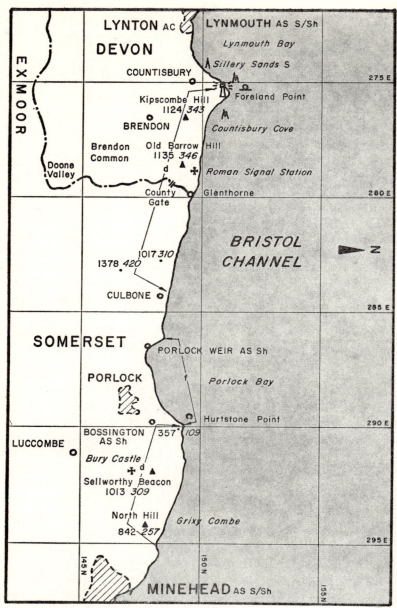

Minehead to Lynton

channel to the lighthouse island of Flat Holm and the steep-walled bird sanctuary of Steep Holm, some 18 miles away. Northwards it is only 12 miles to the nearest point of Wales, the industrial flats of Glamorgan backed by the hill ranges around the coal valleys. By the upper tracks we reach the hill top where there are car parks accessible by road from Minehead. The lower tracks on the seaward face of the hill lead to Greenleigh Farm, where there is a path down to the sands, and on past the slight ruins of Burgundy Chapel, where the route turns inland and climbs to join the others on the hilltop. It is also possible to walk on the beach from Minehead and there seems no reason why the experienced coasteer should not continue on as far as Bossington Beach. Care is advisable over the tides, as there is no public escape route up the cliffs for some $3\frac{1}{2}$ miles. There are a number of steep combes on the seaward slopes of the cliffs, of which Grixy Combe below East Myne is said to be the finest.

The Path continues along the hill ridge between a half and one mile from the sea's edge, rising gradually to Selworthy Beacon (1,013ft). Half a mile to the south is the circular camp of Bury Castle and beyond it the 'artists' dream village' of Selworthy. Between the Beacon and the Castle an access road for cars leads to a car park convenient for short local explorations. The Path continues to Bossington Hill, gradually converging on the coastline again towards Hurlstone Point, where the cliffs 'hang over the beach in a manner peculiarly awful and sublime'. This is usually written 'Hurtstone', but in fact the former is more likely as it was named for an occasion when the Devil stood here hurling stones across the valley to Porlock Hill, where they can still be seen at White-stones. It is possible to go out to the Point to see the natural arch at Gull Rock (or Hole), or there is an alternative right of way across the base. We go down now to the picture village of Bossington—'preeminently', says Harper, 'a hamlet of chimneys'—and so to Porlock.

PORLOCK (SS8846). On A39 which leaves it by the notorious Porlock Hill (1 in 4). Nearest station—Taunton (30m). E.C. Weds. Centre for the National Trust's Holnicote Estate, for picturesque villages and for walking on Exmoor.

Some 2½ miles separate Hurlstone Point from Gore Point on the far side of Porlock Bay. The coastline, flat with a beach of shingle, is nowadays separated from Porlock Village by close on a mile of meadowland. The Path hugs the sea's edge, though inland there are alternative lines on roads through the village, passing shops, inns, etc. To the west of the bay is the port of Porlock Weir; here we continue beside the gateway of Ashley Combe and climb up through Yearnor Wood which clothes the seaward slopes of another great range of hog's-back cliffs. Within a mile is Culbone with its tiny church, 'in as extraordinary a spot as man in his whimsicality ever fixed on for a place of worship'. It is the smallest complete parish church in England; there is no obvious congregation.

Beyond Culbone the line of the Path has been waymarked in red by the National Park authorities; a track leads on climbing higher and higher past Silcombe and Broomstreet Farms, the latter above 1,000ft. Soon afterwards we cross another track (a permissive route, not a right of way) which leads from a small car park on A39 to Sugarloaf Hill (830ft) where wooded slopes fall steeply to the sea. There are good views up and down the coast and across to Wales. The Path continues westwards past Yenworthy Farm and on to A39 at County Gate, the Somerset-Devon boundary, more than half a mile now from the coastline. Down below, the private valley of Glenthorne plunges steeply to the sea. Sixty years ago this section from Culbone to Glenthorne could be traversed on tracks on the seaward flanks of the hills, crossing Silcombe, Twitchen, Broomstreet and Whiteham Combes. This is all inaccessible nowadays. Of the beach itself Archer has written: 'nothing but a protracted trudge along a wide beach over an endless succession of boulders. Even the scenery is slightly monotonous, as there is little marine erosion; timber grows down the slopes almost to the foreshore, and variety would be slight but for an occasional fine waterfall.'

Having reached the main road at County Gate, the problem for the walker is to avoid using it as much as possible during the next few miles to Lynmouth. The Path crosses the road therefore and cuts off a loop by climbing straight over Cosgate Hill; Old Barrow Hill (1,135ft) between here and the sea, has a circular Roman encampment and a panoramic view of the Bristol Channel. We are now forced to follow the main road for almost a mile until just past the turning to Brendon, where the Path strikes off again to the right along the seaward side of Kipscombe Hill and so arrives behind Foreland Point—a prominent jutting headland of 723ft, with a lighthouse built in 1899. It is possible to go out to the headland using the lighthouse road (permissive, not a right of way), but the route right round close to the cliff edge is considered dangerous. We cross the back of the Point therefore to the cliffs above Blackhead and continue over Countisbury Common to the church at Countisbury.

In this section between County Gate and Countisbury there are tracks on the seaward slopes, used and fully described in the *Thorough Guide* at the turn of the century, and still available though prior permission is required by anyone wishing to enter the grounds of Glenthorne. Harper (1908) described this fascinating cliff section: 'So few and far between are those who come this way, that the track kept open by the occasional explorer who brushes aside the brambles and the branches that bar his path, is almost overgrown by the time the next stalwart forces a passage. Here and there a steep little gorge requires skilful manœuvring; in some places, where the track emerges upon the open, bracken-grown hillside, descending alarmingly, and without a break, to the sea far below, it traverses broken, rock strewn slanting ground, where a slip would send the incautious hopelessly rolling into the water; and at other places all signs of a track are lost.' Here we find Wingate Combe, Desolate Combe, and a gully called Pudleep Girts where the path is carried on a wall built across the glen, Countisbury Cove with an accessible shingle beach, and Coddow Combe full of rocks. Page makes it sound like real mountaineering: 'to call it Alpine is not far-fetched, as it is without the protection afforded to Alpine paths'.

Foreland Point is the first place along this coast where climbing is available. The climber can descend on the east side and traverse westwards round it, passing the four Gun Caverns en route. Beyond at Sillery Sands there is an access path and the beach can be followed on by everyone as far as Lynmouth.

From Countisbury Village the Path again runs into problems in avoiding A39, which here descends the famous Countisbury Hill (1 in 4½) along the edge of the steep part of the cliff, passing on the way Countisbury Camp, which may be Arx Cynvit where King Alfred defeated the Danes in 878. The Path crosses the road to Wind Hill and descends a long ridge to the south of the road towards Lynmouth, being forced to use the road itself and a line to its north in the last quarter mile. Another possible variant is to cross into the valley of the East Lyn and go down through the Watersmeet Estate to sea level.

LYNTON AND LYNMOUTH (SS71/7249). On A39. Steamer services up and down the coast. Nearest station—Barnstaple (19m). E.C. Thurs.

Youth Hostel. National Park Information Centre.

Lynmouth, close to sea level at the mouth of the East and West Lyn Rivers, was the scene of the tragic flood disaster in 1952 following rainfall on an unprecedented scale on the Exmoor hills behind. Stream ways, bridges and waterfront have been redesigned to prevent a repetition. The Rhenish tower on the jetty is modern, replacing that destroyed by the floods. The original was a copy of a tower in the Drachenfels and hid an iron water tank on poles. Once a fishing village, Lynmouth became a resort early in the nineteenth century.

A cliff railway, ingeniously operated by the waters of a cliff-top stream that was once a waterfall, leads on to Lynton 600ft higher. There are paths too up through the woods and the twisting Lynmouth Hill (1 in 4). Visitors should climb Hollerday and Summerhouse Hills for the views, walk in the Watersmeet Estate and visit the striking Valley of the Rocks, the former valley of the Lyn River which flowed on westward to the sea beyond Woody Bay. *See* also the Lyn and Exmoor Museum.

Bibliography

O.S. 1 inch Map Sheets 164 (Minehead) and 163 (Barnstaple)
O.S. 2½ inch Maps Sheets SS74, 84, 94. (Relevant portions of these maps are reproduced on Exmoor National Park Definitive Rights-of-Way Leaflets Nos. 3 Old Barrow Hill-Lynton, and 4 Cosgate-Foreland Point.)
Town guides from Minehead and Lynton and Lynmouth
Walks on North Hill, Minehead (Somerset CC)
Exmoor National Park, Waymarked Walks Vol. 2 (Somerset CC)
Folder Map/Guide *Watersmeet* (National Trust)
Presland, J., *Lynton and Lynmouth*, 1917
Nos. 2, 3, 7, 8, 10, 24, 25, 37, 39 from the General Bibliography

2

LYNTON TO LEE BAY

Woody Bay - Heddon's Mouth - Combe Martin
Ilfracombe

THE coast from Lynton to Little Hangman, immediately east of Combe Martin, lies within the Exmoor National Park, while that from Ilfracombe to Lee Bay and beyond is in the North Devon Areas of Outstanding Natural Beauty. The National Trust owns land at Woody Bay, the Heddon Valley, and about one mile of coast to the west including Trentishoe Down, parts of Holdstone Down and the adjacent coast, Golden Cove at Berrynarbor, and most of the coast between Ilfracombe and Lee Bay. The cliffs between Lynton and Combe Martin provide one of the outstanding rock-climbing centres of the West Country. Here in the 1950s C. H. Archer and C. R. Agar carried out an extensive programme of exploration which resulted in a coasteering traverse many miles long of the shoreline at the cliff foot. The cliffs here are hog's-back types with the hill summits only half a mile or so inland, reaching over one thousand feet. Except for the deep cleft of the Heddon Valley the cliff line is unbroken and there are no very marked indentations until we get to Combe Martin.

The rocks are Lower and Middle Devonian. In detail the formations are the Lynton Beds, the Hangman Grits, the Ilfracombe Beds, and the Morte Slates—the second predominantly sandstone, the others slates—the transition points being Woody Bay, Little Hangman, and a point just east of Lee Bay.

This coast was the subject of a scholarly geomorphological study more than fifty years ago by E. A. N. Arber (see Bibliography). He realised the importance to his investigations of a traverse along the beach, but did not have the technical expertise to carry it out. It was left to Archer and Agar to explore the recesses and in particular the great waterfalls which plunge in places over the cliffs. The most notable of these are at Hollow Brook below Martinhoe, North Cleave Gut, Neck Wood Gut, and Holelake below Trentishoe Down, and Sherrycombe below Great Hangman. It is difficult in

25

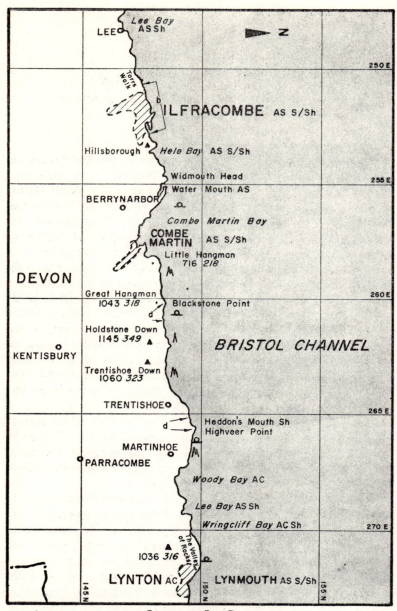

LEE

Lee Bay
AS Sh

Torrs Walk

b

ILFRACOMBE AS S/Sh

Hillsborough

Hele Bay AS S/Sh

Widmouth Head

BERRYNARBOR

Water Mouth AS

Combe Martin Bay

COMBE MARTIN AS S/Sh

Little Hangman
716 *218*

DEVON

Great Hangman
1043 *318*

Blackstone Point

Holdstone Down
1145 *349*

KENTISBURY

Trentishoe Down
1060 *323*

TRENTISHOE

BRISTOL CHANNEL

d

Heddon's Mouth Sh
Highveer Point

MARTINHOE

PARRACOMBE

Woody Bay AC

Lee Bay AS Sh

Wringcliff Bay AC Sh

The Valley of Rocks

1036 *316*

LYNTON AC

LYNMOUTH AS S/Sh

250 E

255 E

260 E

265 E

270 E

145 N   150 N   155 N

N

Lynton to Lee Bay

places to appreciate the scale of the scenery. Looking down from the paths on the flat upper slopes, North Cleave Gut, for example, appears as an almost insignificant cleft in the convex lower hillside. The explorers on the beach found it to be 100yd long, 10yd wide, with rock walls of 250 and 400ft on either side.

By the Path, Lynton to Hunter's Inn is 5½ miles, Hunter's Inn to Combe Martin 6½ miles, Combe Martin to Ilfracombe 4½ miles, 1 mile through Ilfracombe and finally 2½ miles on to Lee Bay— a total of 20 miles.

The Path leaves Lynton by the seaward slopes of Hollerday Hill. After a mile it is forced inland into the famous Valley of Rocks by the steep precipices of Castle Rock which fall vertically to the shore. Beyond is a narrow path down the cliff face to the sand and shingle of Wringcliff Bay. We continue westwards on a minor road past Lee Abbey—the coast at Duty Point is not accessible—to Lee Bay, bounded on its far side by Crock Point. Here, says Harper, there was a landslip in 1776 when cultivated fields slid into the sea, possibly on account of local digging for china clay. The road continues through woods to Woody Bay and Inkerman Bridge, which dates from the Crimea. There is access to the beach and a small waterfall. Woody Bay, formerly Wooda, was threatened with development as a resort in 1895, but fortunately nothing came of it.

The Path follows a broad track (part of the old coach road) contouring high up on the seaward slopes of the hills below Martinhoe, first crossing Hollow Brook (which has been likened to Yoredale in Yorkshire), then passing the site of a Roman signal station on top of the 800ft Beacon Hill. The alternative line here at a lower level is no longer considered safe. The headland below is Highveer Point and beyond is the tremendous Heddon's Mouth Cleave, a cleft down to sea level between 800ft hills less than a mile apart. It would be possible, by mountaineering, to descend direct to the little shingle beach with its ruined limekiln and to climb out again by a trackless rocky hillside up to Trentishoe. The Path however turns south and contours the hillside in a descending line to Hunter's Inn. In this section between Lynton and Heddon's Mouth there is no possibility of using the beach for a route; it has indeed been traversed but is for experts only, extremely complex and offering considerable difficulties.

From Hunter's Inn the Path follows the road westwards, soon turning off however on the very minor road up Trentishoe Combe. Before long we turn to the right and, keeping inside the National Trust property, contour the hills, first above Heddon's Mouth Cleave then passing at length round to the seaward slopes of the cliff. In this commanding position we continue at the same level for some miles along the hog's-back cliffs below the high hills of Trentishoe and Holdstone Downs. We pass the wide jaws of Bosley Gut, down which the shore can be reached with difficulty, and later on the insignificant-seeming North Cleave and Neck Wood Guts, which are such impressive sights from sea level. The slopes are convex and their lower reaches, with waterfalls, beach pinnacles and so on, cannot be appreciated from here. 'It was in Neck Wood', Burton tells us, 'that the men of Combe Martin used to cut the crooked oak that was used for breast-hooks. They went there in boats and climbed up the precipice to reach the wood, handing down the precious spoils from man to man.' Inland there is a motor road, parallel and only a few hundred yards away.

Between Holdstone Down and Great Hangman is Sherrycombe. There is another copious waterfall here from the cliff edge to the beach, but it can only be really appreciated from the sea or from a shore accessible only to the climber. Eventually the Path will plunge down the bracken- and bramble-covered slopes ahead and cross the stream at the head of the fall. Page says of the slopes above: 'So it is mountaineering now with a vengeance. I have done some of the worst of the Lake mountains, I have done Ben Nevis, but I know nothing, except perhaps the screes of Rosset Ghyll, to equal the tremendous climb up the slippery slopes of the Great Hangman. The gradient is about one in two, and you will find it necessary to pause very frequently under colour of admiring the view . . . '

The cliffs below the summit are slashed with the great gash of Great Hangman Gut. Blackstone Point to the east has scars and tunnels of old mine workings. Page found one adit which 'opened on the face of a precipice seven hundred feet high'. The walls on the west of the Gut qualify as the highest sea cliffs in the West Country; close on 800ft sheer they certainly surpass the so-called High Cliff by Crackington Haven, often accorded this honour. We continue dropping all the time towards Little Hangman. The beach below, known as the Rawns, which is only accessible with difficulty, was in fact visited frequently years ago by local women in search of laver, an edible seaweed. There is climbing nearby on Yes Tor. The conical Little Hangman is a splendid viewpoint looking down on Wild Pear Beach, which can be reached by a steep path. A broad track descends along the cliff top to Combe Martin, not actually a right of way but permissive since an agreement was made many years ago between the owners and the Parish Council.

COMBE MARTIN (SS5747, 5846). On A399. Nearest station— Barnstaple (12m).
National Park Information Centre. E.C. Weds.
A long single street 1½ miles in a valley bottom giving on to a sand and shingle beach. A market garden centre noted for strawberries. Mining for silver began here in the reign of Edward I; later other metals were taken, but none for the last hundred years. The church has a striking 100ft tower. *See* also the inn known as the Pack of Cards, of unusual design.

The Path coincides with the road for half a mile before breaking out again on a track on the seaward side, again part of the old coach road. Soon we reach Small Mouth with beach and caves. The Path rejoins the road for a short distance, then comes Watermouth Castle (built 1825) and the long inlet of Water Mouth, which has been likened to a Scottish loch. The outer wall of this is being breached by the sea which has already cut off Sexton's Burrow at the end. Burrow Nose outside the wall gives some rock climbing; there is a cave here also. The Path continues close to the road above the inner wall of the inlet past Widmouth Head, Samson's Bay with caves and fossils, and Rillage Point. Next comes West Hagginton Beach, famous for the variety of its rocks, and so we come to Hele. The bulky Hillsborough (447ft) separates us from Ilfracombe. There is a bird's-eye view of the town from the summit, which in 1900 could be reached on a donkey for a shilling. Below are the tiny coves of Rapparee and Larkstone, the latter named for the ballast, some of which used to be dumped there by foreign ships.

ILFRACOMBE (SS5146, 51/5247). On A361 and A399. Nearest station—Barnstaple (12m). Steamer services up-channel, across to Wales, and to Lundy and Clovelly. E.C. Thurs.

The major resort of North Devon was named in Saxon times, and sent eight ships to Edward III at Calais. Later replaced as a port by Bideford and Barnstaple. The site is enclosed by hills—Hillsborough (447ft) to the east, The Tors (500ft) to the west, and Cairn Top (511ft) on the south. There are several small beaches and fine cliffs. The harbour is sheltered by Lantern Hill, possibly at one time an island, surmounted by the ancient chapel of St Nicholas, a minor lighthouse. Further west on the front is Capstone Hill (156ft), again, maybe, a former island. Do not fail to visit Lundy.

We leave Ilfracombe by the Torrs Walk, where formerly a toll was exacted from the indignant traveller. Now it is National Trust and free. Breezy open cliffs lead on to Lee Bay. Along this section from Combe Martin the alternative route on the beach, though not offering the superlative difficulties of the earlier part of this section, is still for experts only.

Bibliography

O.S. 1 inch Map Sheet 163 (Barnstaple)
O.S. 2½ inch Maps Sheets SS44, 54, 64, and 74. (Relevant portions of these maps are reproduced on Exmoor National Park Definitive Rights-of-Way Leaflets Nos. 1, Trentishoe-Combe Martin, Wringcliff-Trentishoe, and 3, Lynton-Wringcliff.)
Town Guides from Combe Martin and Ilfracombe
Folder Map/Guide *Woody Bay and Heddon's Mouth* (National Trust)
Bowring, D. Warrell, *Ilfracombe Through the Ages*, 1931
Pincombe, L. C. L., *The Call of Chambercombe*, 1951
Nos. 2, 3, 7, 8, 10, 24, 37, 39, 42 from the General Bibliography

3

LEE BAY TO PEPPERCOMBE

Bull Point - Morte Point - Mortehoe - Woolacombe
Baggy Point - Braunton - Barnstaple - Bideford - Instow
Appledore - Northam - Westward Ho!

THE whole of this area falls within the North Devon Areas of Outstanding Natural Beauty. The National Trust has several coastal properties between Morte Point and Baggy Point, as well as owning the seaward slopes of the hills immediately west of Westward Ho! Part of Braunton Burrows is a National Nature Reserve. This is a diverse coastline, for there is a sharp change of direction at Morte Point where we turn from travelling parallel to the beds to a direction cutting across them nearly at right angles. Now the softer beds make beaches and estuaries, the harder the upstanding head-lands between. From Lee Bay to Woolacombe the cliffs are in the slates of the Morte Beds of the Middle Devonian. Various strata comprising the Upper Devonian follow. The Pickwell Down Beds emerge at Woolacombe Beach, the sandstone Baggy Beds from Baggy Point, then the Pilton Beds take us on round to the blown sand of Braunton Burrows. Beyond the Taw-Torridge Estuary, the Culm Measures of the Lower Carboniferous stretch ahead for many miles into Cornwall.

At the Estuary the Path is discontinued, turning inland and stopping at Braunton in the north, starting again further on at Westward Ho! In between, the traveller has the problem of cross-ing these two major Devon rivers, the Taw first bridged at Barn-staple and then the Torridge likewise at Bideford. At low water the combined channel between Braunton Burrows and Northam Burrows is only 220yd wide, but the coastal walker is hardly likely to be equipped with a suitable vessel (as his counterpart in East Anglia might be), nor will he have the local experience essential for even so short a voyage. The only reasonable possibilities are—train or bus from Braunton to Barnstaple, thence bus to Bideford and bus to Westward Ho!, or perhaps leaving the Barnstaple-Bideford bus at Instow to cross on the ferry to Appledore and on from there.

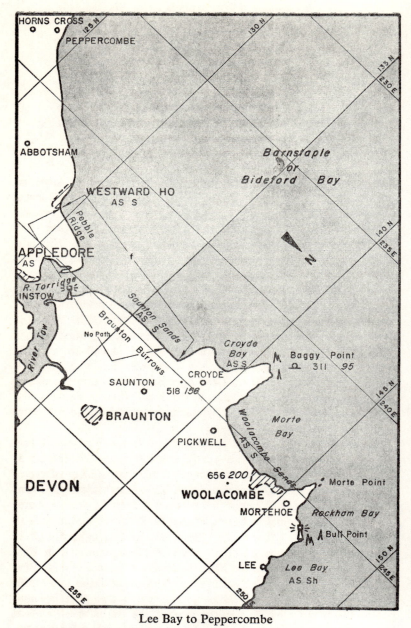

Lee Bay to Peppercombe

(Based upon the Ordnance Survey Map, with the sanction of the Controller of HM Stationery Office, Crown Copyright reserved)

By the Path, Lee Bay to Woolacombe is 4½ miles, Woolacombe
to Braunton is 10 miles and Westward Ho! to Peppercombe 5½
miles—a total of 20. For the hiatus, the detour by Barnstaple and
Bideford is 17 miles, which can be cut by the Instow to Appledore
ferry to 14 miles.

The Path leaves Lee Bay and its small rocky beach by the minor
road westwards, passing soon through a gate on to the open tops of
Damagehue Cliffs. Offshore is Pensport Rock. We soon reach Bull
Point, where there is a lighthouse built in 1879; the lighthouse road,
as usual not a right of way, connects this with Mortehoe. The slate
rocks of Bull Point are curiously light in colour—'glaucous
coloured', says the *Thorough Guide*. Lundy is near at hand and
on fine days Worms Head in Gower can be seen thirty miles away.
The Path hugs the coast round the edge of Rockham Bay, famous
coasteering terrain where Longstaff was climbing in the last century,
and runs out along the peninsula of Morte Point, a turning point
in the coast where the direction changes from east-west to north-
south. The cliffs are hog's-back types, only vertical for the first
few feet above the sea.

The wide bay between here and Baggy Point is backed by the
two-and-a-half mile beach of Woolacombe. On the way down to
it we pass Barricane Beach, entirely made, it is said, from sea shells.
Page could quote some of the exotic shell types, but they will
mostly have gone by now. For a space the road cannot be avoided.

MORTEHOE AND WOOLACOMBE (SS4545 & SS4543). Woolacombe
is on B3343. Nearest station—Barnstaple (12m). E.C. Weds.
Woolacombe is a modern resort beside the fine sands. Mortehoe,
older, on the hill above, has an ancient church.

The Path runs along the slopes behind the sands, but it is equally
possible to walk on the sands themselves or even in the water.
Slowly we come up to the Baggy Point peninsula. The spectacular
rock scenery is hidden beyond the end of the headland, where there
are two beach pinnacles accessible only to the climber, and a great
sheet of sandstone slabs. The first climb here was made by
Longstaff some eighty years ago, and is now receiving intensive
exploration at the hands of modern experts. A network of caves

honeycombs the point, explored of recent years by C. H. Archer and his friends; some were known even in Page's day.

The Path ambles gently back along easy slopes on the south side of the promontory to the sands of Croyde Bay, another first-class beach for children. After a brief encounter with the road we cross behind the sands and press on to Saunton Down, which is traversed by a road on its seaward slopes. Ingeniously the Path manages to avoid all but a few yards of it. Close at hand are two erratic boulders, deposited here by ice thousands of years ago, one 70 cubic feet of red granite probably from Scotland, the other 18 cubic feet of grey granite. Above Saunton Sands is a very large hotel.

For three miles southwards stretches the delightful expanse of Saunton Sands, backed by an extensive dune area, around a mile wide, known as Braunton Burrows. A National Nature Reserve has been created here to preserve the form of the dune country (some dunes reach 100ft) and the prolific vegetation—'800 varieties of wild flower', says Harper. At the south end flows the combined Taw and Torridge, now close to the sea. There are two minor lighthouses, one of which used to be movable to take account of the shifting position of the harbour bar. Page could report a ferry from here to Instow but this no longer functions to save much of the detour. The Path indeed is forced to turn inland along the back edge of the Burrows and so due east to Braunton.

BRAUNTON (SS4836). On A361. Nearest station—Barnstaple (6m). E.C. Weds.

An old town of narrow streets. Here is the largest enclosed field in England, over 350 acres. The church is outstanding. Centre for the sands at Saunton and natural history studies in the Burrows.

BARNSTAPLE (SS55/5632/33). On A39 and B.R. branch from Exeter. E.C. Weds.

Not on the Path but a useful centre for shopping and communications. Situated at the first crossing of the River Taw; the bridge dates back to 1350. The town has a long history, having received its charter from Athelstan in 928, sent ships to the siege of Calais and ships against the Spanish Armada. See St Peter's Church with twisted spire, St Anne's Chapel, the Pannier Market, the

Page 35 Bude, Cornwall (looking S). Taken from Northcott Mouth looking over the characteristic lines of reefs and pinacles (the one called Horn of Plenty is prominent) to the sands of Bude Haven with Compass Point beyond

Page 36 Stepper Point and Pentire Head, Cornwall (looking E). From the Merope Islands across Stepper Point (daymark) and the Camel Estuary to Pentire Point and the sands of Polzeath, with (far off) the coast by Tintagel

Guildhall, Royal Barum Ware Potteries, the Penrose and Horwood Almshouses, Queen Anne's Walk and two museums.

BIDEFORD (SS44/4526/27). On A39. Nearest station—Barnstaple (9m). Boat service to Lundy. E.C. Weds.

As for Barnstaple, but at the first crossing of the River Torridge, the famous bridge dates to the thirteenth century. Here, too, historical connections going back to Saxon times. Features prominently in Charles Kingsley's *Westward Ho!*, written in the town. *See* the parish church (Norman font, etc), the quay and Chudleigh Fort.

INSTOW (SS4730). On A39. Nearest station—Barnstaple (5½m). Ferry to Appledore. E.C. Weds. Youth hostel.

APPLEDORE (SS4630). On minor road from Bideford. Nearest station—Barnstaple (12m by road). Ferry to Instow. E.C. Weds. Boating and one-time fishing village dating back to Saxon times. A small shipbuilding industry. Sandy beach.

NORTHAM (SS44/4529). On A386. Nearest station—Barnstaple (10½m by road). E.C. Weds.

Nearby, King Alfred fought the Danes in the ninth century. Early church.

WESTWARD HO! (SS4329). On minor road from Bideford. Nearest station—Barnstaple (11m). E.C. Weds.

A modern resort with fine sands, caravan parks and holiday camps. The famous golf course was one of the first in England. An outstanding feature of the coast here is the pebble ridge (the Popple), 2 miles long, 50ft wide, 20ft high, formed from stones carried along from the coast to the west.

Whichever way the traveller takes for the detour he should begin his route once again beyond the golf course at the extreme tip of Northam Burrows if only to look back over the narrow channel which has cost so much effort to pass. We set out southwards along the impressive banks of the Popple with high cliffs looming in the distance only a few miles to the south. In places hereabouts the local council are caging the pebbles in wire mesh to fight against erosion. We pass along the beach and reach the restarting of the Path where the cliffs begin to rear in hog's-back form once again.

First come the fossiliferous shales of Abbotsham Cliffs, then after about a mile and a half Greenacliff, where a coal seam on the

C

face of the cliff was worked for a time in 1805. The next headland, Cockington Head, reaches over 350ft. At the base is Tut's Hole, a fine anticline which was reported by Arber in 1903 as 50ft high and 70ft across the base, but distintegrating. The Path continues by the cliff edge past Portledge to the steep little valley of Pepper-combe, which lies half a mile below Horn's Cross on A39. There is a steep access lane to the small shingle beach. An outlier of red Triassic rocks here is the only one for many a mile.

Since Westward Ho! the coast has been swinging gradually westwards, so that by now it is almost east and west again.

Bibliography

O.S. 1 inch Map Sheets 163 (Barnstaple) and 174 (Bude)
O.S. 2½ in Maps Sheets SS44, 43, 42, 32
Town Guides from Barnstaple and Bideford
Balfour, H. Stevenson, *The History of Georghan and Croyde*, 1965
Bidgood, R. F., *Two Villages—Mortehoe and Woolacombe*, 1969
Blackwell, A. E., *The Charm and History of Instow (with Lundy Island)*, 1948
Goaman, M., *Old Bideford and District*, 1968
Nos. 2, 3, 7, 8, 10, 24, 37, 39, 42 from the General Bibliography

4

PEPPERCOMBE TO COMBE VALLEY

Buck's Mills - Clovelly - Hartland - Hartland Point
Hartland Quay - Marsland Mouth - Morwenstow

THIS section, which includes some of the most impressive and most savage cliff scenery in the West Country, lies wholly within the contiguous North Devon and Cornwall Areas of Outstanding Natural Beauty. The National Trust owns small areas at Clovelly and at East Titchberry by Hartland Point, the Vicarage Cliff and Hawker's Lookout at Morwenstow and part of the valley at Duckpool. The rocks are sandstones and shales of the Culm Measures (Upper Carboniferous), but 'squeezed, broken and contorted, like putty in the hands of a giant. It may be doubted', says Arber, 'whether any other shore line in Britain furnishes as many and as perfect examples of folded and contorted rocks as these.' The edges of the various strata, worn down to sea level, run out as reefs across the beach and expose the complexity of the folding. 'Each beach', wrote Charles Kingsley, 'has its black field of jagged shark's-tooth rock which paves the cove from side to side, streaked with here and there a pink line of shell sand, and laced with white foam from the eternal surge, stretching in parallel lines out to the westward, in strata set upright on edge, or tilted towards each other at strange angles by primeval earthquakes.' The first few miles of cliff as far as Clovelly are hog's-back types, the remainder are all flat-topped.

Hartland Point marks another abrupt change of direction in the coast and a dramatic change in fetch. The north-facing cliffs, covered with prolific and largely impenetrable vegetation, rise above the short seas of the Bristol Channel; round the corner the rocks are bare and battered by the long rollers of the Atlantic Ocean. Once again we owe to Arber the elucidation of the local geomorphology. There are numerous waterfalls of streams draining both types of cliff. Notable are the vertical Litter Water near Marsland Mouth, which falls direct to the beach, and the complex series of falls at Speke's Mill Mouth, where changes in course are deter-

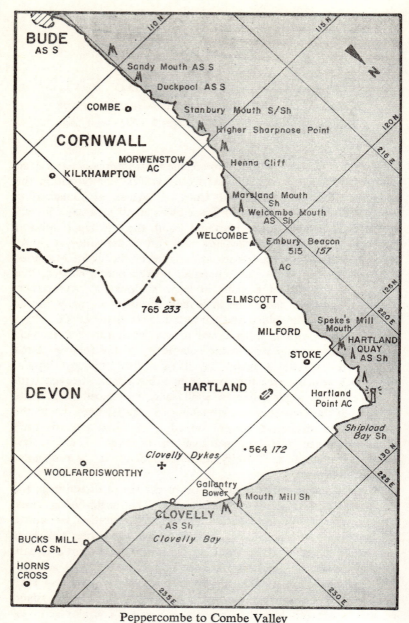

Peppercombe to Combe Valley

mined by the succession of strata across which it flows. Another curious feature of this coast arises from the erosion of the side walls of former valleys running parallel with the sea. A breach in the upper reaches of such a valley provides a new path to the sea for the valley stream and this accounts, as we shall see, for certain flat streamless areas, for example near Hartland Quay, where Wargery Water has been successively diverted.

The west-facing coast is a rock climbing area of minor importance, developed by K. M. Lawder and E. C. Pyatt about ten years ago. There are no major towns and the cliffs between the minor roads or lanes of approach are likely to be found deserted.

By the Path, Peppercombe to Clovelly is 5½ miles, Clovelly to Hartland Point is 7 miles, Hartland Point to Marsland Mouth 7½ miles and Marsland Mouth to Combe Valley 4½ miles—a total of 24½miles.

Between Peppercombe and Buck's Mills the hog's-back cliffs are of easy slope and covered with vegetation. At first the Path hugs the edge; later it turns inland a short way, before running down the end of a ridge past the site of an ancient camp to the seaward end of Buck's Mills. This section can also be done on the beach at low water.

BUCK'S MILLS (SS3523). At the end of a minor road leaving A39 at Buck's Cross. Nearest station—Barnstaple (17½m).
A village in a narrow valley which ends abruptly with a drop to the sea; path to shingle beach. The ruins of the mills remain; the original waterfall was diverted for them. Boyle says it should be spelt 'Bucksh'.

Beyond the village the cliffs are similar. A notice-board beside the beach path advises against climbing on them, but at the same time invites free use of the shore. It is indeed possible to take an alternative route to Clovelly along the shingle, passing waterfalls and a natural arch on the way. The Path however follows the cliff top and in a mile joins the Hobby Drive, a scenic motorable trackway through private grounds which runs from Hobby Lodge on A39 to the top of the street at Clovelly. There is a fee for cars which includes parking at the far end; there is also a fee for pedestrians.

The route, which was so named because it was a hobby of its originator, runs high up along the wooded slopes of the cliff with only occasional glimpses of the sea, bringing us in three miles to:

CLOVELLY (SS3124). On a minor road leaving A39 at Clovelly Cross. Occasional steamer service to Ilfracombe and Lundy. Nearest station—Barnstaple (20m).

One very steep cobbled street, pedestrians only, from cliff top (huge car parks) to tiny harbour. Also Land Rover service to harbour on private road. *See* cottages and flowers. (Timing is an important element. If you wish to study man's reaction to his environment, this is a particularly pleasant one and you will find, in the season, large numbers of reacting visitors. If it is the environment itself you wish to see, the visit should be made in early morning or late evening or out of season altogether.)

The National Trust's Mount Pleasant with wonderful sea views is only a few yards from the Hobby Drive car park. A short distance on, a five-barred gate gives access to the next part of our route. At present it is permissive and not a right of way. After a few fields we find ourselves once again in the woods on top of the cliffs. The Path is clear and straightforward to the top of Gallantry Bower, just over a mile from Clovelly. This is a vertical cliff close on 400ft high; 'venturesome folk', says the guidebook, 'lie flat on the grass and look over, but this is not recommended'. Well-marked paths continue beyond the summit into a wooded valley which leads down to the tiny cove of Mouth Mill and the curiously stratified pinnacle of Blackchurch Rock 80ft high, pierced by two arches. There is access to this point from the National Trust property of Brownsham on the cliff above. The section between here and Clovelly can be done on the beach, Arber tells us, at a suitable state of the tide.

'Wild scrambling', says Harper, 'is the portion of him who would explore the coastline between here and Hartland.' The Path will hug the cliff edge most of the way looking down on steep walls or slopes of impenetrable vegetation. In Page's day the way out of Mouth Mill was 'a difficult climb through a coppice of low weather-beaten oaks, under the branches of which you sometimes have to creep on all fours'. The Path should give somewhat easier going.

First comes Windbury Head, with a camp, then Brownsham Cliff, then Exmansworthy Cliff, which gives a fine view back to Black-church Rock and Gallantry Bower. Past Gawlish Cliff, we reach Shipload Bay where there is a good path down to the sand/shingle beach and some contorted strata to see on Eldern Point. Nearby is East Titchberry Farm (National Trust) with a car park. For the last half mile to Hartland Point the cliff edge route is cut off by radio installations and we are forced to join the minor road built for the lighthouse. This cliff section (Mouth Mill to Shipload Bay) could also be taken on the shore, but it is a serious undertaking because of the lack of escape routes on the cliffs between. Three miles away inland is:

HARTLAND (SS25/2624). Reached by a network of minor roads north-west of A39. Nearest station—Barnstaple (23m). E.C. Tues. In pre-Beeching days it claimed the distinction of being the English town farthest from a railway. It is the only place within reach of many miles of this lonely coast.

Hartland Point, Ptolemy's 'Promontory of Hercules', seeming to Defoe 'a mountain-like proboscis', is another abrupt turning-point in this coastline. The lighthouse built in 1874 stands on a shelf 100ft above the sea. Behind it the Point reaches 350ft; 'to get upon it', says Page, 'one must scale an Alpine-looking col—a feat only to be attempted when there is little or no wind, as the edge is only about a foot wide'. Now we fence it off! Lundy is only about twelve miles away to the west; we look out from here over the wide fetch of the Atlantic Ocean.

The Path turns southwards hugging the cliff edge most of the way. The pinnacle of Cow and Calf is followed by Upright Cliff, a huge smooth face of rock. Smoothlands nearby is part of the original valley of Titchberry Water, which now reaches the sea further north. Hereabouts marine erosion has worn away some of the softer strata to form a tunnel. The route continues over Blegberry Water and Black Mouth, where a somewhat larger stream from Hartland Abbey comes down, to the high contorted cliffs of the Warren. The pinnacle of Bear Rock on the foreshore, twin flakes of rock side by side and some eighty feet high, gives a rock climb for experts only. There are other pinnacles, as well as reefs and caves. Much of this foreshore south of Hartland Point can be traversed on foot at low tide with only an occasional scramble; exits are available where the streams come down, while the rock climber can ascend the cliffs themselves in places without too much difficulty. We have now reached:

HARTLAND QUAY (SS2224). At the end of a minor road from Hartland. Nearest station—Barnstaple (26m).
Maton, in 1794, found 'a dozen decent cottages and a commodious little pier'. The quay has gone, the habitations are converted to a hotel (with a swimming pool). *See* St Nectan's Church at Stoke with 128ft tower, half a mile inland.

Characteristic flat lands on the cliffs to the south of Hartland Quay mark the former line of Wargery Water, which has found the sea successively north of Hartland Quay, between Hartland Quay and Screda Point, south of Screda Point and now just north of St Catherine's Tor. The sea has eroded away half of this conical hill formerly surmounted by a camp. The next stream, Milford Water, drops to the sea at Speke's Mill Mouth in a complex four-part fall. There is a shingle and rock beach, reached by cars at great danger to their suspension and sumps by a rough track from Lymebridge. Brownspear Point to the south has some climbs, while somewhere hereabouts, says Pearse Chope, is a deep cave called Moll Davey's House.

The next cliff section is very wild and little visited. We pass Longpeak, and by the edge of Milford Common and by Mansley Cliff (over 500ft now) to Sandhole Cliff, where a few hundred yards have to be taken on the minor road between Elmscott (where there is a Youth Hostel) and Welcombe. The Path soon breaks away again to the cliff edge, reaching 453ft by Nabor Point and then 515ft at Embury Beacon (camp); after Knaps Longpeak we descend to sea level at Welcombe Mouth, which is accessible by very minor roads from A39. Now it is a mere half mile over another hill or by the beach to the Devon/Cornwall border at Marsland Mouth, another shingle beach to which there is no road access. Off the next headland and accessible along the rocky shore is the 'dark and ugly-snouted' Gull Rock, the first of many so named along the Cornish coast. It may be just accessible at very low water, but only to the rock climber. In the cove behind is the impressive 70ft fall of Litter Water. The Path continues along the cliff edge, past Yeol Mouth where there is another climbers' crag, to the bulky mass of Henna Cliff, which rises to 450ft above the famous church and vicarage of:

MORWENSTOW (SS2015). At the end of a minor road off A39. Nearest station—Barnstaple (29m).
A scattered hamlet with ancient inn and fine church, associated with Rev R. S. Hawker, prolix writer and eccentric churchman of the last century. On Vicarage Cliff nearby is his hut or lookout, where he wrote and received his inspirations while watching the seas. The place is named for St Morwenna, whose well was down the face of the cliffs.

Below Hawker's Lookout is a climbers' crag. He missed seeing the first climb on this great out-jutting promontory by about a hundred years. At the south end of the beach below is Higher Sharpnose Point with another crag and a coastguard lookout, below which the Tidna stream makes another interesting fall. The beach at Stanbury Mouth, the first coming this way to show any considerable amount of sand, is only accessible by a non-motorable trackway. Until a few years ago the Path would have had to make a substantial detour here, because anti-aircraft guns used to be fired out to sea from the cliff top. These military installations have now been abandoned but the site is undergoing extremely ugly development as a satellite-tracking station. However we can continue by the cliff edge. We pass above the huge vertical ribs of Lower Sharpnose to the Combe Valley. There is a sandy beach and access by a minor road.

Bibliography

O.S. 1 inch Map Sheet 174 (Bude)
O.S. 2½ inch Maps Sheets SS32, 22, 21
Chope, R. Pearse, *Farthest from Railways*, 1934
idem, *The Story of Hartland*, 1902
Nos. 2, 3, 6, 8, 10, 24, 37, 39, 42 from the General Bibliography

5

COMBE VALLEY TO TINTAGEL

Bude - Dizzard Point - Crackington Haven - Cambeak
Boscastle - Tintagel

EXCEPT for some five miles of more or less urban area attached to Bude, all the coast described in this section falls within the Cornwall Area of Outstanding Natural Beauty. The National Trust has several properties on or near the coast—an area near Dizzard Point, the headlands on either side of Crackington Haven and the coast on southwards for three miles, Boscastle Harbour and at Tintagel, Barras Nose, Glebe Cliff, Penhallick Point and the Old Post Office. The castle at Tintagel is in the care of the Ministry of Public Building and Works.

Bude has extensive sands which stretch from Combe Valley to Bude Haven, then reappear at Widemouth. The cliffs provide plenty of variety. The Culm Measures of the Upper Carboniferous are continuous and flat-topped from Combe Valley to Rusey Beach below High Cliff and show the twisted and contorted strata we have seen further north. After Millook Haven the cliff faces have been modified by landslipping. On towards Boscastle the Lower Carboniferous outcrops in hog's-back type cliffs—mostly black shales, but with sandstones, cherts and prominent veins of quartz. Beyond Boscastle the rocks are Upper Devonian. Along this stretch of coast are numerous pinnacles and islands. Once again we owe much of our knowledge to the work of Arber, who should be read in the original by the keen coastal walker.

Leland, reporting to his King on the state of the country in the early sixteenth century, wrote: 'From Stratton to Padstow the Contery by the North Se ys rather Hylle then Montaynenius, and ys very fertyle of Gras and Corne; and the Clives of the sayd Northe Se betwne the Places aforsayd hath good fyne blew Slates apte for Howse Kyveryng, and also hath diverse Vaynes of Leade and other metalles not yet Knowen.'

By the Path, Combe Valley to Bude is 3½ miles, Bude to Crackington Haven 9 miles, Crackington Haven to Boscastle

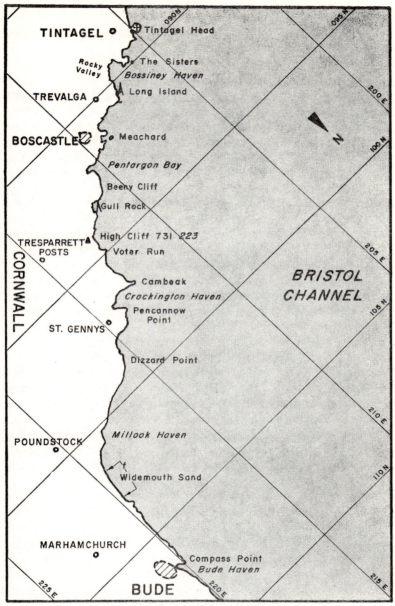

Combe Valley to Tintagel

(Based upon the Ordnance Survey Map, with the sanction of the Controller of HM Stationery Office, Crown Copyright reserved)

6½ miles and Boscastle to Tintagel 4½ miles—a total of 23½ miles.

After a short distance over boulders and reefs it is possible to walk all the way from Combe Valley to Bude on the sands below half tide. The Path continues by the cliff edge and one can interchange in many places. It is a mile to Sandy Mouth, which can also be reached by a minor road. Arising from the sands are three diverse pinnacles—the Square Block squat and bulky, and the Flame taller and pointed, near the centre of the beach, and round the northern corner, Ship Ashore, perhaps more like an awkwardly-shaped submarine. All give rock climbs. Three quarters of a mile ahead the beach pinnacle at Northcott Mouth is called the Unshore Rock, or Smooth Rock; there is road access here also. Between Northcott and Bude is the famous Maer Cliff, often figured in textbooks of geology to illustrate folded rocks, and two more pinnacles —one called Horn of Plenty because it offers so many handholds to the climber, the other Easy Street because it is (comparatively) easy to climb. The cliffs behind are mostly steep and bewilderingly stratified.

BUDE (SS20/2106). On an A road a mile off A39. E.C. Thurs. 'Britain's Bondi', an important resort with no promenade but extensive sands. To the south is Compass Point with a tower and a view. The Bude Canal, formerly thirty miles long, now has only a short length navigable. The tidal range here is around twenty feet, so that there can be impressive high seas at spring tides—'here can be seen waves mountains high, and the roar, as they break and pound the foreshore, can be heard for miles inland'.

The Path climbs to Compass Point and we look back along the high coast to Henna Cliff and Lundy. Ahead, where the coast curves round towards the west, is Trevose Head, with nearer at hand the outjutting Cambeak and the large hotel perched prominently on the cliffs by Tintagel. Tors on Dartmoor and Bodmin Moor are also included in the clear view. The Path crosses Efford Beacon and follows the cliff edge with the road never very far away. There are reefs, buttresses, and pinnacles on the shore, which can be reached in places. In two and a half miles we reach the broad sands of Widemouth, which the walker will prefer to a slog through the car parks. The prominent Black Rock, variously described as sandstone, schist, and lava, is haunted by the wrecker Featherstone, 'whose howls can be heard when the nights are dark and stormy'. In places by Wanson Mouth (said to be a small-scale model of Boscastle harbour) and along Penhalt Cliff the Path uses a steep little minor road; we descend finally to Millook Haven, notable for the extremely contorted strata in its cliffs.

Steeply up again on the far side to Millook Common, we embark on a section of landslipped cliff which extends to Dizzard Point and beyond. The Path follows the edge of the landslipped area so that it is sometimes as much as a quarter of a mile from the sea's edge. Below at first is Concleave Strand, then in about a mile and a half we reach Dizzard Point, five hundred feet high, its seaward slopes covered with trees. It is another quarter of a mile to Chipman Point, from which we can look down into the steep-sided wooded valley of Scrade Water, ending in a waterfall to the beach of Cleave Strand. Nearby is Stoneivy Rock, prominently quartz veined. The next valley, that of Coxford Water, is also of interest. It is another steep-sided cleft ending in a waterfall, but here the sea is eroding not only the valley mouth but also the north wall, so that we see an advanced stage of the process of the diversion of a stream by coast erosion, which we have observed elsewhere. Half a mile up this valley the ancient church and vicarage of St Gennys recall those of Morwenstow similarly sited. St Gennys, it is said, was beheaded: 'he bowed to the executioner, picked up his head and walked away'. The Path climbs the south wall of the valley on to Pencarrow Point, strikingly contorted and veined, and descends on its far side to Crackington Haven. According to Arber the beach can be reached at a number of points between here and Millook, but it is likely that a traverse would be both involved and difficult.

CRACKINGTON HAVEN (SX1496). Reached by minor roads from either Tresparrett Posts or Wainhouse Corner on A39.
A small secluded resort with fine sands and striking rock scenery.

Rather than take a short cut it is worth while to go out, as does the Path, to the promontory of Cambeak, 'a gruesome place', says Folliott Stokes, 'so narrow the head, so sheer the precipice'. It is indeed a short scramble out to the farthermost tip, a magnificent viewpoint for all this coastline from Hartland Point to Trevose Head. The next section of cliff is once again landslipped. The beaches, the Strangles and Rusey divided by the rocks of Voter Run, are accessible by paths. There are pinnacles, notably Samphire Rock on the Strangles and another larger but nameless by Voter Run; Northern Door still joined to the land by the uppermost rocks shows the intermediate arch stage of stack development. The Path climbs steadily up to High Cliff (731ft), 'mouldering precipices', says Harper, 'of mingled buff and purplish blue'. This may be the highest in Cornwall, but it is unimpressive, separated from the shore by hummocky slopes of landslip. The man who wrote 'adventurous souls like to lie face down on its edge and gaze at the sea, over 700ft below' can never have been there. A byroad from A39 which crosses Tresparrett Down (861ft) and descends to Crackington Haven is only a quarter of a mile away. At Rusey we change from Upper to Lower Carboniferous. Past Buckator, a steep cliff of black slate, is another Gull Rock, large, square-topped, detached and apparently inaccessible. We continue round Beeny Cliff, the Beeny Sisters foaming out to sea, and by Fire Beacon Point into Pentargon; the road B3263 is very close at this point. There is a cave on the east of the cove where the cliff is remarkably steep. At the back is another fine waterfall over the black cliffs, of which Thomas Hardy wrote: 'The small stream here found its death. Running over the precipice, it was dispersed in spray before it was half way down, and falling like rain upon projecting ledges, made minute grassy meadows of them.' Half a mile on over Penally Hill is Boscastle. The Meachard offshore was cut off from Penally Point by the sea, which is now working the same process on the end of the Point. There are blowholes hereabouts.

BOSCASTLE (SX0990/91). On B3263. Youth hostel. E.C. Thurs. Leland described it as 'a pore Havenet of no certaine Salvegarde'. The narrow and tortuous harbour, picturesque but looking impossible to navigate, is said to resemble Balaclava. Fine centre for cliff walks. *See* also: Forrabury Church, Forrabury Common with strip field cultivation going back to Saxon times, the Cobweb Inn, and the Valency Valley.

The walk from Boscastle to Tintagel is fine and easy to follow, though at the turn of the century the *Thorough Guide* found it 'almost impossible except after long drought and when the corn is cut'. The headland of Willapark (317ft; camp) forms the south side of Boscastle harbour. The Path skirts this and continues round West Blackapit, 'a ghastly chasm in the black cliffs . . . with a sheer drop of some hundreds of feet into the sea, which can he heard thudding in caves invisible'. We soon reach Ladies Window Head, named for a curious aperture in the summit rocks through which there is a view of the cove below. Offshore is Short Island, while round the corner rises the 200ft stack of Long Island, detached and not readily accessible. The bay ahead is Bossiney Haven where there is sand and swimming. The Rocky Valley running up from here to the main road and beyond merits a diversion. On the shore is a rock arch known as Elephant Rock; offshore is the 'spiny' Lye Rock. The Path continues to a second Willapark (305ft; also with camp); rocks called the Sisters lie offshore. Only half a mile remains to Barras Nose and Tintagel Head with its castle ruins, approached over a neck of rocks. Above this, wrote Norden, 'the ascente is by a verie rockye and wyndinge waye, up the steep sea-clyffe, under which the sea waves wallow, and so assaylethe the foundation of the Ile as may astonish an unstable brayne to consider the perill, for the least slipp of the foote sendes the whole bodye into the devouringe sea . . . Under the mayne Ilande, and through it from cliffe to clyffe, is a cave or vaulte, so spatious and capable as a fisher boate may pass from one syde to the other.' On the adjacent cliff is King Arthur's Castle Hotel, which has been a landmark for the last twenty miles.

TINTAGEL (SX0588) (actually Trevena). On B3263. Youth hostel. E.C. Weds.
Bleak, unattractive village half a mile from the sea. The castle is a place of pilgrimage for tourists. The present ruins are of a twelfth-century castle, the inner ward on the headland, the outer on the mainland, formerly linked by a drawbridge; previously the site was occupied by a Celtic religious settlement. Tradition

links Tintagel with King Arthur, but there seems to be no direct evidence of this. At times and seasons when visitors are few the Ministry of Public Building and Works will most certainly still have the gates open. *See* also: Merlin's Cave, King Arthur's Hall (modern), the Old Post Office (fourteenth century) and the church of St Materiana on the cliff.

Two and a half miles inland a road over the summit of Condolden Barrow reaches 1,009ft.

Bibliography

O.S. 1 inch Map Sheet 174 (Bude)
O.S. 2½ inch Maps Sheets SS21, 20, SX19, 08
Town Guide from Bude
Nos. 2, 3, 6, 9, 20, 21, 28, 39, 41, 47, 48 from the General Bibliography

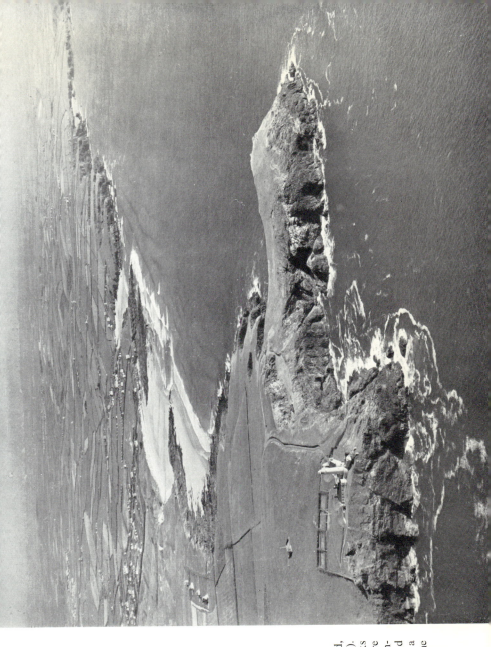

Page 53 Trevose Head, Cornwall (looking S). The lighthouse marks the Head. Beyond are the sands of Constantine, Treyarnon and Porthcothan with a distant glimpse of the 'Cornish Alps'

Page 54 Cape Cornwall, Cornwall (looking NE). A mine chimney marks the summit of the Cape. This 'mining coastline' of Botallack and Levant ends at Pendeen Lighthouse. In the far distance is the promontory of Gurnard's Head

6

TINTAGEL TO TREVOSE HEAD
Trebarwith Strand - Port Isaac - Pentire Point - Padstow
Trevose Head

TINTAGEL HEAD is a turning point in the coastline, which in the usual pattern starts southwards and gradually curves round until running westwards again at Trevose Head. The whole of this great arc lies within the Cornwall Area of Outstanding Natural Beauty. The National Trust has a reasonable foothold here with properties as follows—at Treknow Cliff above Trebarwith Strand, the coastline between Tregonnick Tail and Jacket's Point including Tregardock Beach, several small sites at Port Gaverne, the whole of the peninsula comprising Pentire Point, Rumps Point and Cliff Castle and several small sites between here and Portquin.

The rocks are mostly slates and shales of the Upper and Middle Devonian with various included igneous rocks. The latter are often most resistant to weathering and form outstanding coastal features. There are igneous rocks at Trebarwith, then a coast of fairly uniform slates runs on to Port Isaac. Stepper Point, Rumps Point, and Cliff Castle on the mainland are all greenstone, as are the offshore islets of Gulland Rock, Newland, and the Mouls. Portquin lies between lava headlands; Varley Head is in slates; Pentire Point, Cataclews Point, Porthmissen Point and Trevose Head are all igneous. At Pentire Point the pillow lavas, so called because of the detailed shape of the outcropping rock, are impressive and indeed famous. The bays are cut in the softer shales between and there are several fine sandy beaches.

The Camel Estuary is the first big break in the Path since the Taw-Torridge. Fortunately there is a convenient and active ferry from Rock to Padstow and the paths on either side of the estuary which are followed to reach it enable the walker to see the surf beaches of Polzeath, the important geological site at Trebetherick Point and the little port of Padstow. The Camel would be an important anchorage were it not for the Doom Bar, a great sandbank stretching from Daymer Bay across towards Hawker's Cove,

D   55

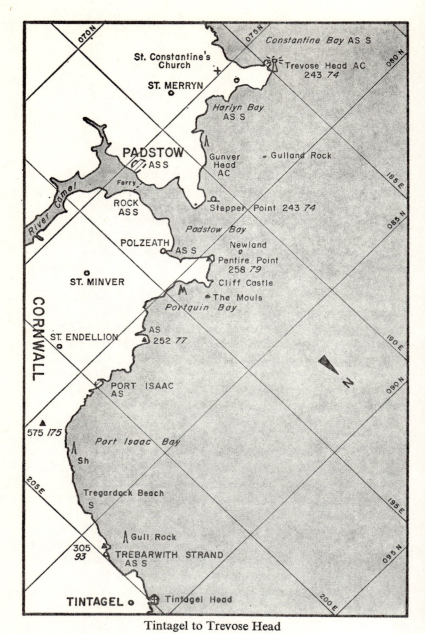

Tintagel to Trevose Head

(Based upon the Ordnance Survey Map, with the sanction of the Controller of HM Stationery Office, Crown Copyright reserved)

which blocks it but for a narrow channel. A large amount of sand is taken continuously from the Estuary for agricultural purposes.

By the Path, Tintagel to Port Isaac is 9 miles and Port Isaac to Rock 10½ miles. The ferry crossing of just over half a mile leads to a final section from Padstow to Trevose Head of 9 miles—a total walking distance of 28½ miles.

The track in the little valley coming down to Tintagel Cove and Head, churned considerably by the Land Rover service for unwilling walkers, is slowly being distributed over the valley vegetation. We climb away towards the church at St Materiana sited in a position of maximum exposure on the cliff above. The Path leads on easily over Treknow Cliff, passing a fine pinnacle in a quarry on the way, to Trebarwith Strand, which has a sandy beach with caves and an access road from B3263. Offshore the third Gull Rock rises steeply conical to 133ft; Folliott Stokes is alone in calling it Otterham Rock. At the south end of the beach is Dennis Point (305ft) with a very steep crag; the Path contours this on the landward side, only to be confronted with the deep valley above Blackways Cove. After a mile along the cliff edge we come to Tregardock Beach (National Trust) where there are sands reached by a path over a landslipped cliff face. This point can be reached also by a footpath from Tregardock Farm (road access nearby).

At this point Old Delabole Quarry is only about two miles away inland—just beyond B3314 and the disused railway. This unsightly, but quite striking, piece of man-made landscape has been claimed as the largest single open excavation in England. It is a vast hole in the ground having a diameter of a quarter of a mile and is several hundred feet deep. Operations began between three and four hundred years ago and still continue.

Returning to the coast we proceed through National Trust property for a mile as far as Jacket's Point. The Path continues up and down crossing a series of small valley mouths and the headlands between to Bounds Cliff, below which is a 50ft pinnacle, the Filly Horse. The byroad to Port Gaverne begins to converge on the cliff edge, but the Path manages to stay clear of it all the way to the village, a former port, now preserved by the National Trust. More or less contiguous is:

PORT ISAAC (SW9980). Approached by B3267 off B3314. Nearest station—Bodmin Road (15m). Bus service. E.C. Weds.

Fishing port since the fourteenth century. Delabole slates were shipped from here before the days of the railway a hundred years ago. Now a small resort with a shingle beach. Narrow streets.

Hockin rates the next coastal stretch from here round Pentire to Polzeath 'one of the grandest, wildest and most stimulating in Cornwall, compared with Kynance to Gunwalloe and Treryn Dinas to Land's End.' Between Port Isaac and Portquin (2½ miles ahead) the Path follows the cliff edge round Lobber Point to Pine Haven and will one day (we hope) continue round Varley Head, Scarnor Point and Kellan Head; between them are pleasant little coves whose sides are coated with luxuriant vegetation. At present we follow a direct footpath between Pine Haven and Portquin, which itself is never more than a quarter of a mile from the sea. Between Kellan Head and Rumps Point lies Portquin Bay; at this side immediately below us is the narrow slit of Portquin Harbour with Cow and Calf Rocks offshore at the entrance. Legend has it that this was a thriving fishing port until all the menfolk were killed in a storm disaster at sea; thereafter it was abandoned. Yet the anchorage looks hardly big enough for a fishing fleet, while Norden in 1584 already described it as 'all decayed since the growing up of Port Isaac'. The west shores of the harbour have a tradition of exclusion of the public from the cliffs. Thus sixty years ago Folliott Stokes could write that this and Prussia Cove were the only places in the hundred miles between Marsland Mouth and the Lizard where the public was forbidden by a private owner to use the coast path. Hockin in the 1930s had difficulty here also. Now we are to have a cliff-edge path all the way with exciting views ahead to the igneous rocks of Rumps Point and the Mouls.

The almost rectangular peninsula of Pentire Point jutting out to the north-west is all National Trust property; 'a wildly beautiful region', says Harper, 'the cliffs honeycombed with caves'. We come first to Com Head, which at present has the distinction of providing the only rock climb recorded anywhere along the North Cornish coast between Bude and St Ives. This state of affairs is somewhat artificial, because of the reluctance of climbers these days to give away the whereabouts of anything new and interesting. There are plenty of possibilities, both behind and ahead, but if they have been done they remain unrecorded. Rumps Point, which might well be part of a mountain ridge with a succession of rock pinnacles, just misses being a rock climb. There is a camp and some caves. The conical islet of the Mouls offshore reaches 159ft. Pentire Point is the other seaward corner of the rectangle; this nearly vertical eastern portal of the Camel Estuary reaches 258ft and commands a fine view over this great waterway backed by the line of St Breock Downs. The rock scenery is impressive with steep buttresses of pillow lava, which look very suitable for the rock climber. The islet of Newland, half a mile out, is 122ft.

Stepper Point, the western portal of the Estuary, is stepped back exposing the eastern shores immediately by Pentire to the Atlantic rollers. Thus there is surfing on the magnificent sands at Polzeath. Here, says Betjeman, 'caravans, railway carriages, shacks and bungalows have done their worst, so that one has continually to look out to sea and at National Trust property to remember Old Cornwall'. At Trebetherick examination of the Pleistocene shore deposits produced, during 1943, a classic account by Arkell of the geomorphological history of beaches in southern England. We pass Daymer Bay and the Doom Bar, St Enodoc with its famous golf course and ancient church (once buried by sand and then restored), and come at length to Rock. The ferry here was an ancient route, for there is a record of its use as long ago as the fourteenth century. Of nearby Porthilly Norden wrote: 'Between this hauen and another coue called Portkerne passeth a great cave which they call an Ogo, under a mighty rocky mountayne, throwgh which holl or cave the sea ebbeth and floweth, as the fishermen ther affirme near haulfe a myle in length.' But Portkerne is Port Gaverne and is five miles away! We cross the ferry to:

PADSTOW (SW9175). Reached by A389 branching from A39 two miles from Wadebridge. Nearest station—Bodmin Road (16½m). E.C. Weds.

There has probably been a port here for more than 1,000 years. Padstow sent ships to the siege of Calais and against the Armada. Leland noted 'a good quick fisher town but uncleanly kept'. In more recent times it has been engaged in fishing and ship-building, *Murray's Guide* (nineteenth-century) noting 'an anti-

quated unsavoury fishing town'. Now a pleasure resort with sands
and boats in the estuary. *See*: St Peter's Church, lifeboat, harbour, the hobby horse dances on May Day.

The Path leads back towards the mouth of the river by Harbour
Cove and Hawker's Cove past the Doom Bar again and on to
Stepper Point (243ft), where there is a white daymark 40ft high.
The *Thorough Guide* describes a boat trip round this coastline,
probably the only way to see the fine caves, Pepper Hole and
Butter Hole, which are round the corner from Stepper Point, and
Seal Hole in Seal Cove further on by Gunver Head. 'None but
swimmers can explore Seal Cove, but to them we know of no
experience more out of the common run.' The Path, safely on
the cliff top, passes Gunver Head and almost immediately arrives
at the savage rock scenery of Tregudda Gorge, the cleft between
Lower Merope Island and the main cliff. Middle and Higher Merope
Islands further out look equally inaccessible; the *Thorough Guide*
from its boat sees one of these as Queen Elizabeth. One and a half
miles out is (nearly the fourth Gull Rock) Gulland Rock.

Continuing westwards we pass Porthmissen Bridge, with two
natural arches, the so-called Marble Cliffs formed of alternate
layers of slate and quartz and Round Hole, a blow hole opening
on the cliff top, and so reach Trevone with sands and road access.
Next comes Harlyn Bay with the same amenities, and a large
caravan site, plus a museum of antiquities collected in a local
Celtic burying ground discovered in 1900. Beyond Cataclews Point
(caves) is Mother Ivey's Bay (sands) with the access road to the
lighthouse close at hand. Merope Rocks on the north side have
arches and caverns. Nearby is quarried the famous Cataclews Stone,
described by Betjeman as 'the only slate which can be deeply
carved, it is of blue-grey colour and has a look of cast iron'. Trevose Lighthouse was built in 1847. This is a major turning point
and could in fact be considered as the centre of a long coastline
which can be divided into two bays, one from here to Hartland Point,
the second from here to Godrevy Point by St Ives. The clear view
should encompass both these, the night view their two lighthouses.

Bibliography
O.S. 1 inch Map Sheet 185 (Newquay and Padstow)
O.S. 2½ inch Maps Sheets SX08, SW97, SW87
Nos. 3, 6, 9, 20, 21, 28, 39, 41, 47, 48 from the General Bibliography

7

TREVOSE HEAD TO PERRANPORTH
St Eval - Bedruthan Steps - Newquay - Holywell Bay
Perranporth

THIS section is a popular holiday district and includes Newquay, the major resort of Cornwall, as well as many lesser resorts. Though there is some interesting cliff scenery, notably at Bedruthan Steps and Holywell Bay, the beaches are likely to have a much greater concentration of holiday-makers than we have met before. The first few miles from Trevose Head to Bedruthan Steps are included in the Cornwall Area of Outstanding Natural Beauty. The remainder is all part of the urban area of Newquay and its satellites and was therefore considered unsuitable for designation. Trethias Island by Treyarnon Beach is a Nature Reserve. The National Trust holds a series of coastal properties: at Porthcothan, Park Head and Diggory's Island at the north end of Bedruthan Steps and Pendarves Point at the south end, several properties around the Gannel at Newquay, Kelsey Head, Holywell Beach and a small islet called the Chick further south.

The rocks are mostly slates and shales of the Upper and Middle Devonian with some grits, sandstones, and conglomerates. The bays are often carved in the shales, the headlands between being either rocks locally hardened, as at Kelsey Head, East and West Pentire Points, or igneous intrusions, as at Park Head, which is greenstone. There are numerous stacks and islands. The Gannel Estuary south of Newquay is interesting as a drowned river valley reminiscent of Water Mouth near Ilfracombe (Chapter 2). Blown sand occurs in places, notably at Penhale and Gear Sands behind Perran Beach, where it reaches a height of 225ft, Holywell Bay, and Constantine Bay. Ancient buildings have been buried and uncovered again by these shifting sands. At Penhale Sands also we come across the first signs of Cornish tin-mining, deserted engine-houses and chimneys on lonely cliff tops, which thenceforward will appear increasingly as we move westwards.

By the Path Trevose Head to Bedruthan Steps is 7 miles, Bed-

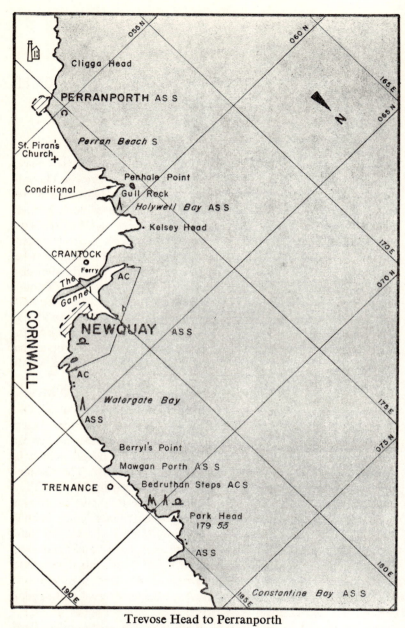

Cligga Head

PERRANPORTH AS S

Perran Beach S

St. Piran's
Church

Conditional

Penhale Point
Gull Rock
Holywell Bay AS S

Kelsey Head

CRANTOCK
Ferry

The
Gannel

AC

b

NEWQUAY   AS S

AC

Watergate Bay

AS S

Berryl's Point

Mawgan Porth AS S

Bedruthan Steps AC S

TRENANCE

Park Head
179 55

AS S

Constantine Bay AS S

CORNWALL

N

055 N

060 N

055 N

070 N

075 N

165 E

170 E

175 E

180 E

190 E

195 E

Trevose Head to Perranporth

(Based upon the Ordnance Survey Map, with the sanction of the Controller of HM Stationery Office, Crown Copyright reserved)

ruthan Steps to Newquay 6½ miles, then 1½ miles through urban Newquay. Newquay to Holywell Bay is 6½ miles and Holywell Bay to Perranporth a further 4 miles—a total of 25½ miles.

One mile west of Trevose Head are the reefs called the Quies; there is another Round Hole in the cliffs above Mackerel Cove. From here the coast runs due south and we soon come to the first of the many sandy beaches, Booby's Bay and Constantine Bay. On the cliff top is Trevose Golf Course and among the dunes the half-buried ruins of St Constantine's Church. Immediately afterwards comes Treyarnon Beach with Trethias Island, the Nature Reserve. There is a Youth Hostel nearby. Next we pass several narrow inlets divided by narrow tongues of land; there are caves sometimes used by seals and the marks of a camp. Minnows Cove is divided into two sections by a cone-shaped peninsula; access between them is possible at low tide through a natural arch. Minnow Islands are on the foreshore. There are sands at Porthcothan Bay with arches and tunnels on the south side; Trescove Island lies on the foreshore and on the main cliff nearby are the remains of a funnel hole, the seaward side of which has been eroded away. The Path continues to hug the cliff edge, though it seems clear that an alternative route could be made along the shore in many places with frequent opportunities for interchange. We soon reach the outjutting greenstone headland of Park Head, National Trust property and the beginning of the outstanding stretch of coastline, one and a half miles long, known as Bedruthan Steps.

The Steps are named for the succession of rocky islets along the foreshore which are said to have been stepping stones for the giant Bedruthan. The name became transferred to the flight of steps—'ancient beyond knowledge', says Harper—cut down the cliff face at the south end and giving access to the beach. A few years back these were closed after a boy was killed by a rock fall and there is now no way down except for a rock scramble on material of dubious quality suitable only for the experienced coasteer.

The National Trust's Park Head property includes several small coves and a rock arch, six round barrows and Diggory's Island, the first of the 'Steps', where there are caves and arches. The next

'Step' is the famous Queen Bess Rock; Folliott Stokes considered the profile unfeminine, but by way of consolation found one much more feminine among the crags nearby—the rediscovery of this is left as an exercise for the student! A long beach of fine sand connects together these various rocks; the next is Samaritan Rock, named presumably for the *Good Samaritan* wrecked here in the last century. So active were the wreckers on this occasion that Bodmin Gaol is said to have been full afterwards with St Eval men.

ST EVAL (SW8769). Access by minor road from St Columb Major on A39. Nearest station—Newquay (7m).
An extensive aerodrome site, 1½ miles from the coast. The church was rebuilt in the eighteenth century as a daymark for mariners.

Back at the 'Steps', Redcove Island comes next with **Red Cliff Castle** on the mainland above, then beyond where the steps used to be, Pendarves Island. A cave here provides a tunnel through to the next cove, at the far side of which is the conical peninsula known as Carnewas Island. Now half a mile ahead are the wide sands of Mawgan Porth, with caves on the northern side.
The next headland is Berryl's Point, followed by Griffin Point, where there is a promontory fort. This is the northern limit of the two-mile stretch of sand known as Watergate Bay; at the south end is Trevalgue Head (Fort and barrows), which is Newquay. The Path follows the edge of the cliffs which are of black shale and 200ft high in places; eventually it has trouble in staying independent of a parallel minor road. Horse Rock and Zacry's Islands, with caves and tunnels, are at the south end of this beach, which can easily be used as an alternative to the Path when the tide is low.

NEWQUAY (SW80/8161 etc). Accessible by A roads from various directions—A392, A3058, A3059 and A3075. BR branch line from Par. Airport, services to London and the Scillies. E.C. Weds.
Formerly a fishing village, by the 1890s a rising watering place, now Cornwall's largest and best equipped resort. Extensive sands. In Newquay Bay between Trevalgue Head and Towan Head— a range of beaches including Towan, Great Western, Tolcarne,

Crigga, Lusty Glaze, and St Columb Porth Beaches. In Fistral
Bay between Towan Head and East Pentire Point—Fistral Beach.
See: Harbour; Huer's House (whence a lookout scanned the
sea for pilchard shoals); Towan Head (a natural pier); the Island
(a rock on Towan Beach reached by a bridge); Bishop's Cave at
Crigga Point; Porth Island (Trevalgue Head) also reached by a
footbridge, with round about—Mermaid's Cave, Blowing Hole,
Banqueting Hall Cave (200ft long and 60ft wide), Cathedral
Cavern (partially destroyed by a rock fall), Infernal Regions
Cave, Fern Cave, Boulder Cavern. The caverns beneath Towan
Head are no longer accessible.

The traveller on the Path now crosses the Gannel, either by ford,
haunted it is said by the cries of one who was drowned here, or
ferry, depending on the state of the tide, and continues behind the
sands of Crantock Beach to Pentire Point West. Legend has it
that inland around Crantock was the one-time district of Lan-
garrow, a veritable Cornish Sodom, which in due course was
destroyed for its wickedness by fire and storm and buried finally
under the sand dunes. Beyond the cove of Porth Joke rises Kelsey
Head with a cliff castle and the National Trust's 'Chick' close at
hand offshore. Holywell Beach with more extensive sands is
enclosed between here and Penhale Point opposite, the latter surmounted by a mine chimney (Wheal Golden). The holy well is at
the east side of the beach. Our fourth Gull Rock is out in the bay,
while rising from the sands are two striking pinnacles—one bulky
and dark coloured, the other slender and light. One of them is the
Monk, probably the former, but authorities are not completely in
agreement. Inland here is blown sand.

Beyond Penhale Point is the extensive dune area of Penhale
Sands, the first two miles of which form a firing range. Even when
this is not in use the route close to the sea past Ligger Point to the
dunes towards Perranporth is not permitted officially. When the
danger signals are displayed the traveller must follow cart tracks
and footpaths behind the dunes by Ellenglaze, Trebisken, Mount
and Gear, returning to the edge of the beach by way of St Piran's
Church (site marked by large white cross). Eventually the dunes
give place to dark-coloured cliffs honeycombed with caverns, and
so we come to:

PERRANPORTH (SW7553). Accessible by B3285 off A3075. Nearest station—Truro (9½m). E.C. Weds.

Fine sands, with archways, caves and pools. *See*: St Piran's Church (above) 2 miles NE (built in the sixth or seventh century, covered by drifting sand, excavated and now protected by a concrete outer cover); St Piran's Round 1½ miles E (ancient amphitheatre accommodating 2,000 people).

Bibliography

O.S. 1 inch Map Sheets 185 (Newquay and Padstow) and 190 (Truro and Falmouth

O.S. 2½ inch Map Sheets SW87, SW86 and SW75

Town Guides from Newquay and Perranporth

Husband, S. T., *Old Newquay*, 1923

Nos. 3, 6, 9, 20, 21, 28, 39, 41, 47, 48 from the General Bibliography

8

PERRANPORTH TO ST IVES

St Agnes - Portreath - Gwithian - Hayle - St Ives

THE Cornwall Area of Outstanding Natural Beauty includes all the coastline in this section from a point just west of Perranporth down to Godrevy Towans on the edge of St Ives Bay, excepting only about two and a half miles between Tobban Horse at Porth Towan and Portreath—the industrial complex at Nancekuke. The remaining stretch round St Ives Bay is also excluded because of industrial Hayle. There are some fine beaches, but as a whole this area is not as popular for holiday-makers as that further north and, except for St Ives, there are no large resorts. The National Trust owns St Agnes Beacon, land round Chapel Combe leading down to Chapel Porth by St Agnes, and a splendid stretch of six miles of magnificent cliff scenery on Carvannel, Reskajaege and Hudde Downs between Portreath and Godrevy Towans.

The rocks are chiefly slates, though at Cligga Head we find the first coastal granite. This reminds us that it was the intrusion of the granite into the Cornish rocks which led to the formation of the metalliferous ore bodies, the basis of the mining industry. It is not surprising that the first appearance of granite should coincide with the first major mining area we have encountered on our route. The cliff scenery between Perranporth and St Agnes Head, and onwards, is impressive indeed but the remains of ancient mine workings detract from its beauty. We have to abandon temporarily our interest in natural scenery and derive pleasure instead from a study of the works of man and of the secrets of nature he has dug from the ground. En route we search therefore for crystals and mineral specimens in the spoil heaps.

By the Path, Perranporth to St Agnes Head is 5 miles, St Agnes Head to Portreath 5 miles, Portreath to Gwithian 8 miles and Gwithian to St Ives 6½ miles—a total of 24½ miles.

The Path climbs out of Perranporth over Droskyn Point where mine adits emerge on the cliff face, and on to the granite of Cligga

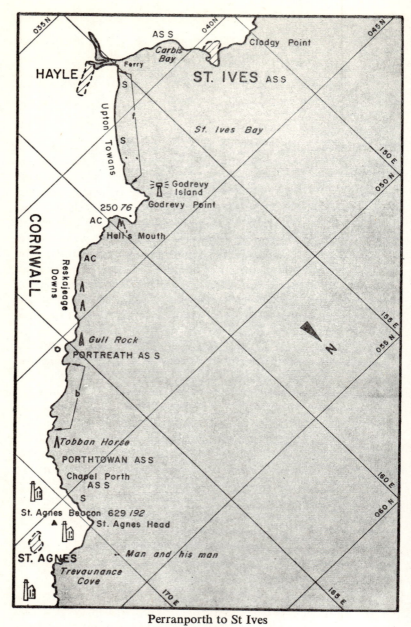

Perranporth to St Ives

(Based upon the Ordnance Survey Map, with the sanction of the Controller of HM Stationery Office, Crown Copyright reserved)

Head, a scene of almost complete devastation. Not only are there ancient mine workings (Wheal Perran, Perran Great St George, Good Fortune, and Cligga) but also the ruined buildings and dumps of Nobel's Dynamite Works, that could hardly look worse if indeed it had blown up. Currently, mining is going ahead once again in these parts. Beyond Hanover Cove, Wheal Prudence Mine rises above the headland of Pen-a-Gader, which is pierced by a slit similar to that in Carn Lês Boel (Chapter 10). Looking back at Cligga, Folliott Stokes comments on the colouring and complexity of the face 'streaked with pink and white and dove greys, honey-combed with old mine adits . . . the lower parts carved into the most fantastic shapes'.

In the next half mile the cliffs reach 300ft. Soon comes the deep valley of Trevellas Coombe with mining relics (Blue Hills, Bowling Green, and Velvas Mines) leading down to the celebrated coloured cliffs of Trevellas Porth. Alongside is Trevaunance Cove, which has a small sandy beach very popular nowadays. This was the site of a miniature harbour from which the local tin was shipped, called by Harper one of the greatest curiosities in Cornwall—'a miniature haven constructed in a most hazardous situation at the foot of the cliffs, and overhung by the crazy old wooden staging and gear of apparatus for loading vessels from the heights'. The guidebook comments specially on the colours here, the sea 'every conceivable shade of blue, green and purple', the cliffs 'rich buffs and browns'. Wheal Kitty and Wheal Friendly are on the slopes above which lead up to:

ST AGNES (SW71/7250). Access by B3285 from Perranporth or B3277 from A30. Nearest station—Redruth (7m). E.C. Weds.
Former centre of a thriving mining area, now centre of a little-known holiday district of moors, seascapes, and sandy coves. The visitor should climb St Agnes Beacon (629ft, ¼m SW) with views to Trevose Head, Brown Willy, the Cornish Alps, Falmouth Harbour, St Michael's Mount, and the hills of West Penwith.

'Trevaunance Cove', says Hockin, 'is Cornwall's nearest match to Devon's Lynmouth with the Beacon towering 600ft above it, but though the rock scenery is much grander than Lynmouth's, and though the lower slopes of the Beacon are not treeless, there is no

hanging forest, and mining has bleached the cliff tops to a desert.'
One and a half miles ahead is St Agnes Head, reached on the Path
by following the cliff edge past Polberro Mine, where, Hamilton
Jenkin tells us, 'in 1750 the treasures of tin being raised proved so
great that sufficient horses could not be found in the whole neighbourhood to carry it to Calenick smelting house', so carts were used
for the first time for carrying the ore.

   Elsewhere he quotes an account from the *Royal Cornwall Gazette*
of 1823 of a party held in the great Seal Hole Cavern in the cliffs
near here. When difficult of access from the shore, this could be
reached by the shaft of North Seal Hole Mine. The party took
tea there and then spent three hours with music and singing. St
Agnes Head is another turning-point in the coast, and from it
we set off again southwards. At first the cliffs are steep and high.
Passing Wheal Coates (National Trust) we reach in one and a
quarter miles Chapel Porth (also National Trust), a valley giving
on to a considerable length of sand with some fine caves. The
next stretch to Porth Towan can be traversed here at sea level, or
we can follow the Path past Wheal Charlotte over the headlands.
At the far end of the beach beyond Porth Towan is a bulky
pinnacle called Tobban Horse.

   Hereabouts we reach the industrial complex of Nancekuke. There
is a high barbed-wire fence along the cliff which the Path (sometimes closed to the public) skirts for the next two and a half miles
to Portreath Harbour, passing at the end a 25ft daymark on the
eastern cliff.

PORTREATH (SW6545). Access by B3300 from Redruth or B3301
from Hayle. Nearest station—Redruth (4m). E.C. Weds.
A small resort with sands and a cave; the fifth Gull Rock is
offshore. There is a small port, still active, whence copper ore
was at one time exported to South Wales.

We have now reached the beginning of one of the finest stretches
of cliff in Cornwall. The cliff top is preserved (we hope), while
the scenery inland has not been spoiled by mining. We follow
a track on the western side of the beach from which the Path
sets out round the seaward slopes of Tregea Hill. Soon afterwards
comes a curious inlet called Ralph's Cupboard with promontories

Page 71 Land's End, Cornwall (looking SE). Near at hand Dr Syntax's Head and the First and Last House, further right the Hotel and Dr Johnson's Head. The line of big granite headlands continues to the south-east

Page 72 Lizard Point, Cornwall (looking NE). The old lifeboat launcher rises from Polbream Cove. The lighthouse is on the most southerly point, separated by Housel Bay from Bass Point with its Signal Station

and stacks. We cross the stream going down to Porth-cadjack Cove
on the far side of which is Samphire Island. A camp surmounts
the next headland with the Crane Islands offshore. The possibilities
of traversing at the cliff foot are unknown, but the difficulties seem
obvious and for experienced coasteers only. The flatness of the
cliff tops is remarkable, mile after mile as though sliced off with
a knife. At length the road begins to converge on the cliff edge
and the Path eventually cannot avoid it. They separate, only to
come together again at Hell's Mouth where there is a car park;
many stop to look over the edge into a savage cove with steep
walls and the sea far below. The road now makes straight for
Gwithian, but the Path continues to hug the coast all round the
Knavocks. It is three-quarters of a mile to Navax Point, passing
the way down to Seal's Hole at the cliff foot described long ago
by W. H. Hudson, and a further three-quarters of a mile to Godrevy
Point. Offshore is Godrevy Island with its unmanned lighthouse,
built in 1859, the first since Trevose Head.

We are now in St Ives Bay and there is a fine view across to
Carbis Bay and St Ives with the hills of West Penwith behind. On
the eastern side of the Bay is an extensive area of blown sand—
Godrevy, Upton, Phillack, and Hayle Towans—with bungalows,
chalets and caravan parks, fronted by long stretches of sand. We
cross the Red River and follow the road for a few hundred yards to:

GWITHIAN (SW5841). On B3301 from Hayle to Portreath. Nearest
station—Hayle (3m).
The ancient St Gothian's Oratory has become reburied in sand
and lost.

Our route follows the junction of the sands and the dunes to the
River Hayle, where at one time the tide flowed to St Erth bridge.
Débris from tin streaming carried down from inland gradually
silted up the estuary to the state we find today. There is a ferry
to Lelant half a mile below:

HAYLE (SW5537). On A30 and BR main line. E.C. Thurs. Youth
hostel at Phillack.
According to *Black's Guide* (80 years ago) 'a dirtier, squalider,
less interesting town is not to be found in all Cornwall'. Now an

E

industrial port with large factories and a power station and no scenic attractions, nor any historical interest.

We cross the ferry (or it is three miles round by road). Lelant on the far side has suffered in the past from blown sand, 'decayed', says one ancient writer, 'by reason of the sande which had choaked the harbour and buried much of the lande and houses'. The present church was in danger at one time, but strategic planting of marram grass has saved the situation. There is a private bird sanctuary in the estuary.

The Path follows the edge of Porth Kidney Sands and continues in close proximity to the railway, past a number of ancient mining sites and Carbis Bay, into St Ives.

ST IVES (SW5140). Access by A3074 from A30 1m W of Hayle and by BR branch line from St Erth. E.C. Thurs.

The 'Capua of Cornwall'. Began to grow in the fourteenth century, developing eventually into an important fishing port. *Murray's Handbook* (1851) says 'most abominably tainted with the effluvia of fish cellars'. By the end of the nineteenth century the artists had arrived and growth as a resort had begun. The town is built on a peninsula (St Ives Head or the Island) facing north-east and up the cliff slope behind. Porthmeor Beach faces north between the Island and Carrick Ddu; the harbour shelters below the south side of the Island; Porthminster Beach faces east between the Island and Porthminster Point (National Trust). The sands of Carbis Bay are contiguous to the south. On the Island was one of Cornwall's earliest lighthouses for, said Leland, 'there is now at the very point of Pendinas a chapel of St Nicholas and a pharos for lighte for shippes sailing by night'. *See*: Parish Church (fifteenth century); lifeboat house, harbour: Huer's House (where a lookout scanned the sea for pilchards; 13 million caught in one day in 1905). *Visit*: Knill Monument; Trencrom National Trust), Trink and Rosewall Hills; the former mining area round Halsetown.

Bibliography

O.S. 1 inch Map Sheets 190 (Truro and Falmouth) and 189 (Land's End)

O.S. $2\frac{1}{2}$ inch Maps Sheets SW75, 64, 54 and 53
Town Guide from St Ives
Bizley, M., *Friendly Retreat* (St Agnes), 1955
Hamilton-Jenkin, A. K., *The Mines and Miners of Cornwall* Vol. 2
   St Agnes-Perranporth, 1962
Nos. 3, 6, 9, 20, 21, 28, 39, 41, 47 48 from the General Bibliography

9

ST IVES TO LAND'S END

Zennor - Gurnard's Head - Morvah - Pendeen - St Just
Cape Cornwall - Sennen Cove - Land's End

THIS last section to Land's End along the north coast, the edge of the granite moorlands of West Penwith, is a real mountain area even though the hills do not reach a thousand feet. Starting at St Ives, the whole of the coastline is included in the Cornwall Area of Outstanding Natural Beauty, while the National Trust owns Hor Point, Tregerthen Cliff, and Zennor Head, Rosemergy and Trevean Cliffs, and Mayon and Trevescan Cliffs at Sennen, as well as a fine example of a Cornish beam engine at the Levant Mine at St Just.

'Between St Ithes and Pendene', says Norden, 'the sea clyffes doe glitter as if ther were muche Copper in them.' In fact the three rock types which make up this coastline are slate and volcanic rocks of the Devonian period, known respectively as killas and greenstone, and granite which welled up from the interior of the earth in Carboniferous times, baking and altering the other two and filling cracks in the strata with metalliferous ores. In some places these hardened rocks form the headlands, while the bays between have been carved in granite, in others there are headlands of pink granite often presenting a characteristic castellated appearance. Outstanding feature of the coast scenery are the zawns, steep-sided clefts going down into deep water which have been formed by the removal of soft strata, often the ore veins, by the action of the sea. Between St Ives and Porthmeor is either killas or greenstone, except for granite at Wicca; it is granite from Porthmeor to Pendeen; slates give rise to a notable mining area between Pendeen and Cape Cornwall; finally there is granite from Sennen Cove to Land's End.

Except for the possibility of reopening some of the tin mines there would not seem to be any serious threat to amenities. Mining in the past has left serious scars, but most of these are tumble-down, overgrown and generally accepted into the landscape, even of interest for their own sakes. The coast is too rugged, the sandy

76

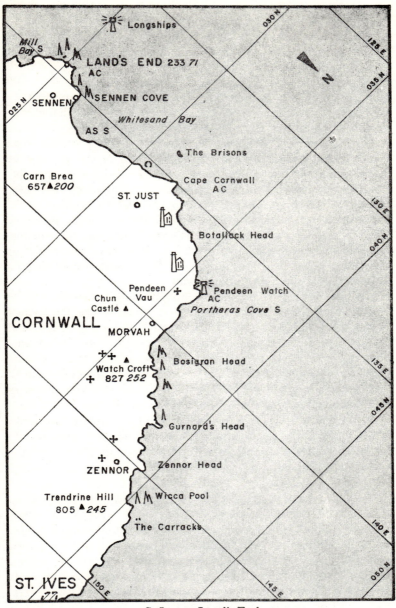

St Ives to Land's End

(Based upon the Ordnance Survey Map, with the sanction of the Controller of HM Stationery Office, Crown Copyright reserved)

coves too small and relatively inaccessible for any pretentious
holiday development, so that the chief amenity is always likely to
be the scenic drive along the coast road, which runs along a shelf
between half a mile and a mile from the cliff edge with far-off
glimpses of the sea. Sennen Cove is the only place where the sea's
edge is approachable by road; Land's End, Cape Cornwall and Pendeen Lighthouse the only places where roads lead to the cliff edge.

This is one of the leading rock climbing areas of the West
Country. Exploration was begun at the turn of the century by
A. W. Andrews, one of the founders of the sport of coasteering.
Progress was slow until the great boom in climbing after the
Second World War. There has been tremendous activity in the
last decade, so that standards now are extremely high. Intending
climbers should consult the climbers' guidebooks (see Coasteering,
Appendix VII), where they can pick out routes appropriate to their
experience. Cliff foot traverses are exceptionally difficult and
walkers should stay firmly on the Path.

The area is rich in antiquities, though these are mostly on the
moors rather than the cliff top. Certainly places like the ancient
British village of Bosporthennis, Mên an Tol, Lanyon Quoit, and
Chûn Castle are worth a diversion, just as it is worthwhile sometimes to get a view of the sea from the moors. The coastwise
traveller is usually confined to the cliff top, hemmed in against
the steepness by the edges of cultivation, but here in wilder country
his domain extends to the summits of the paralleling hills.

By the Path, St Ives to Gurnard's Head is 7 miles, Gurnard's
Head to Pendeen Lighthouse 5½ miles, Pendeen Lighthouse to
Cape Cornwall 4 miles and Cape Cornwall to Land's End 6 miles—
a total of 22½ miles.

The Path skirts Porthmeor Beach at St Ives and climbs up to
Clodgy Point, the first headland really exposed to the Atlantic. For
much of the way it will follow the line of the old Coastguard path
and thus will certainly hug the cliff edge; this has become overgrown
with the years and will need plenty of traffic in the future to keep
it open. The cliffs from Clodgy to Carn Naun are greenstone; seals
are said to disport themselves on the reefs known as the Carracks.
The sixty-foot granite monolith in the cove beyond is called Wicca
Pillar. Next comes the slate and greenstone Zennor Head; from

the sands of Porthzennor Cove on this side a fishing boat used to operate during the last century; at Pendour Cove on the far side a notice-board of historical interest to our present subject has indicated the whereabouts of the coast path for many years now. Half a mile inland is:

ZENNOR (SW4538). On B3306. Nearest station—St Ives (5m). Centre for cliff walks. *See*: Church; Zennor Quoit, and around it 'fantastically shaped rocks in the likeness of anvils, giant loathly toads the size of houses, and things of vaguely inimical outline'; Mulfra Quoit (2m S).

Zennor Consols Mine stood on the next headland; close offshore is Carnelloe Island which has been reached by swimming. Next come two small sandy coves with more ruins on the cliff above, followed by the outjutting Gurnard's Head, greenstone joined to the main cliff by a neck of slate. There is an Iron Age fort. 'The figure of a Sphinx', says W. H. Hudson, 'the entire body lying out from the cliff, the waves washing over its huge black outstretched paws.' There is a path to this point from the main road. In the next cove is a black pinnacle—Pedn Kei (Dog's Head). The granite begins half a mile on at Porthmeor Cove; inland is the hamlet of Porthmeor and beyond that on the moor the ancient village of Bosporthennis. The granite cliffs are low at first but by the time we reach Bosigran Head and Porthmoina Cove the scenery is fine indeed. On the east side of the Cove below the Head are the great verticals and overhangs of Bosigran Face; at one time a huge white patch used to be painted here to enable the lighthouse keepers at Pendeen to estimate the visibility and thus know when to sound the foghorn. On the far side of the Cove a long ridge consisting of a series of pinnacles climbs the cliff from sea to summit, while in between a large pinnacle or island rises from the sea—Porthmoina Island. Around here is the main climbing area and the traveller on the Path may well see climbers in action on one or other of these crags as he passes. The old Count House of Carn Galver Mine, the ruins of which stand out between here and the coast road, is now the West Country headquarters of the Climbers' Club; above it the rough hillsides of Carn Galver slope up to the skyline. A mile ahead is the hamlet of:

Morvah (SW4035). On the coast road (B3306), or access by minor road from Penzance via Madron. Nearest station—Penzance (5½m).

See: Church; Lanyon Quoit (2m SE); Mên Screfys and Mên an Tol (1½m E, below Watchcroft (826ft) the highest hill in West Penwith); Chûn Castle (1m S); Pendeen Vau fogou (1m W).

There is a fine sandy beach at Portheras Cove reached by track and path from Morvah. The Path itself continues along the cliff edge. The western headland of Portheras is Pendeen Watch with a lighthouse built in 1900; a secluded cove with sand can be reached by a steep path down the cliff here and there is a fine view back to the big cliffs round Porthmoina Cove, where the white patch used to be. There is road access to the lighthouse of course from B3306 at Bojewyan. Ahead now is a fine cliff line of metamorphosed rocks with relics of mining on every hand. In particular it is very necessary to look out for the occasional unprotected shaft or tottering wall.

Almost immediately we come to Geevor Mine on the front slopes of the cliffs, one of the few still active in Cornwall today. Just beyond it is the famous Levant Mine, closed since 1930, where a Cornish beam engine is now preserved by the National Trust. This mine produced both tin and copper; the galleries from it were driven out under the sea to a depth of two thousand feet and as much as a mile from the shore. This is what Folliott Stokes found at the turn of the century: 'The situation is a very striking one . . . and has a certain weird grandeur. Its tall chimneys, sheds and tin-washing beds are but a sorry substitute for the heath and golden gorse which their presence has destroyed. Descending the valley, we climb the opposite hill, past mud and miners, arsenic fumes and tram lines till we reach the top . . . a stunted and blasted heath with little dynamite store sheds whose lightning conductors clatter in the breeze, and unsightly refuse heaps of rock and clay.' Probably in those active days the cliff paths, beaten constantly by the miners going night and day to and from work, were well marked and easy to follow. There was a terrible accident here in 1919 when the main lifting shaft of the 'man engine' broke and numbers of miners were killed. All this has long passed and now Nature has largely taken over once again.

A mile further on is Botallack where the ruined engine-houses cling to the bare face of the three hundred foot cliff in a most striking situation. This too produced both copper and tin and here too were tunnels under the sea. It was visited in its heyday by Queen Victoria and Prince Albert and later by the Prince and Princess of Wales, the princes each time descending into the mine. In 1914, says *Black's Guide*, visitors could descend the mine in the morning between 7 and 9 am. The charge was 10 shillings, a high fee indeed! The coast between here and Cape Cornwall has been designated a Site of Special Scientific Interest by the Nature Conservancy. The Path continues at the cliff edge passing the ramparts of Carn Kenidjack and Wheal Edward Mine and leaving Wheal Owles a quarter of a mile inland.

ST JUST (SW3731). On the coast road B3306 and A3071 from Penzance. Nearest station—Penzance (7m). Youth Hostel (1m S). E.C. Thurs.
Centre for cliff walks and mining and mineral studies. *See*: Plane an Gwarry (ancient play and sports enclosure); Carn Kenidjack (1½m NE); Church.

Cape Cornwall, the only 'cape' in England and Wales, juts out almost as far west as Land's End. There is a mine chimney on top and modern mining is continuing close by. Offshore are the Brisons (90 and 71ft), which are mentioned by Drayton in *Polyolbion*. Norden on his maps (1584) shows two other pinnacles in the sea—the Kilguthe and another Gull Rock—which seem to have disappeared in the interim. There is an interesting barrow on Carn Gloose above Priest Cove. We cross the valley of Porth Nanven to Progo, where a natural arch stands on the sands. The Path continues along cliffs which are lower now to Aire Point, where the extensive sands of Whitesand Bay begin. At the far end sheltered under the headland of Pedn Mên Du is:

SENNEN COVE (SW3526). Accessible by minor road from A30. Sennen Churchtown is on A30, 1 mile from Land's End. Nearest station—Penzance (10m).
Small resort, centre for cliff walks and rock climbing. *See*: lifeboat; Huer's Hut.

Land's End is less than a mile now along the fairly level top of the granite Trevescan Cliff. En route we look back at a pinnacle in the sea known as the Irish Lady and the impressive climbers' crag on this side of Pedn Mên Du. Offshore, about $1\frac{1}{2}$ miles, is Carn Bras with the Longships Lighthouse, completed in 1873 and replacing an earlier one of 1795. So we come to Dr Syntax's Head, the most westerly point of the mainland of England, and the so-called 'First and Last House'. Beyond is a conspicuous hotel, difficult to eliminate from the view.

Bibliography

O.S. 1 inch Map Sheet 189 (Land's End)
O.S. $2\frac{1}{2}$ inch Map Sheets SW54, 43, 33, 32
Hamilton-Jenkin, A. K., *The Mines and Miners of Cornwall Vol 1 Around St Ives*, 1961
Matthews, J. H., *St. Ives, Lelant, Towednack and Zennor*, 1892
Nos. 3, 6, 9, 20, 21, 28, 39, 46, 47, 48 from the General Bibliography

10

LAND'S END TO TREWAVAS HEAD

Land's End - Pordenack Point - Tol Pedn Penwith
Mousehole - Newlyn - Penzance - St Michael's Mount
Cudden Point - Trewavas Head

THERE is a break of 3½ miles in this section of the Path, where no line has been designated from Penlee Point by Mousehole through the urban area of Penzance. Almost all the remainder is included in the Cornwall Area of Outstanding Natural Beauty. National Trust properties here include the coast from Nanjizal to St Levan, Treen Cliff, Pedyn y Vounder beach and the peninsula of Treryn Dinas by Porthcurno, Cribba Head, Penberth Cove and valley, St Michael's Mount and Lesceave Cliff at the eastern end of Prah Sands—an impressive holding. The stretch of cliffs in the first seven miles from Land's End is considered by the author of the *Thorough Guide* to be 'equal if not to exceed in grandeur and beauty of cliff scenery any other of equal length in these islands'. 'Happily', he comments, 'the nature of the cliff top is such that it can be fully seen without overtaxing the endurance or the nerves of the least valiant pedestrian.' The great headlands here, particularly Pordenack Point, Carn Lês Boel and Tol Pedn Penwith are the supreme examples of crenellated granite, 'cubes on cubes of it rising sheer as though built by Titans'.

The granite ends at Lamorna; thereafter we find outcrops of slates and greenstone much the same as on the northern coast (Chapter 9). The greenstone tends to form headlands here also, for example at Tater Dû, the Greeb and Cudden Point. St Michael's Mount and Rinsey and Trewavas Heads are, however, outliers of the granite.

The granite cliffs make an important contribution to the West Penwith climbing area, the principal centre being the five great buttresses on Tol Pedn Penwith; Land's End, Pordenack Point and Carn Lês Boel are also important, and there are many lesser. There has been very little mining activity anywhere along this coast, except for some isolated sites by Trewavas Head and Prussia Cove.

By the Path, Land's End to Porthcurno is 5 miles, Porthcurno

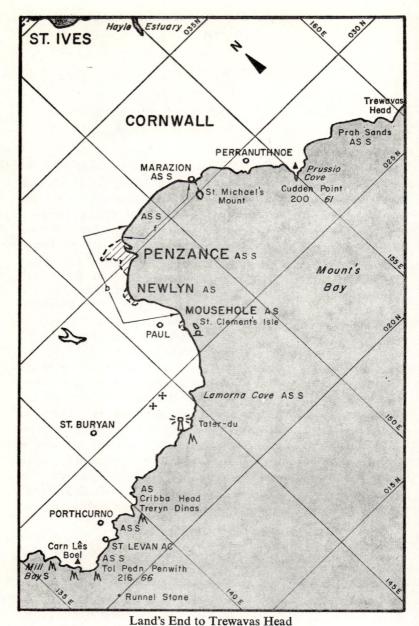

Land's End to Trewavas Head

(Based upon the Ordnance Survey Map, with the sanction of the Controller of HM Stationery Office, Crown Copyright reserved)

to Penlee Point 8 miles. After a 3½ mile gap through the urban area of Penzance, it is 5 miles on to Perranuthnoe and finally 5 miles from Perranuthnoe to Trewavas Head—making 26½ miles altogether.

We have now reached our farthest west, Land's End, the most popular place of pilgrimage in the West Country. Here we may find ourselves once again studying people rather than scenery, for in the season one is cut off from the latter by car and coach parks and the massive hotel. Come by in the evening—the crowds will have gone home and we can stand and watch the sun slide down towards America, knowing there is nothing in between but the hundred odd Isles of Scilly, the flashing lights of Round Island, Peninnis, Bishop, Wolf, Seven Stones and Longships, and legendary Lyonesse.

There are two headlands—Dr Syntax's beyond 'First and Last House', which is the real Land's End, and Dr Johnson's below the Hotel nearest to the end of A30 by which most pilgrims come. There is climbing here and a cave, Land's End Hole, which has to be approached by boat. However the cliffs are neither so impressive nor so typically castellated as those further along the coast to the south, where we will find the now unshared view to be very much the same anyway. Offshore is the rocky island of the Armed Knight (88ft), and soon afterwards close to the cliff rises Enys Dodnan, flat-topped and arched on its outer face. With rare abandon the *Thorough Guide* recommends that it can be 'reached at low tide by those equal to an awkward bit of crag work'. The next headland, Pordenack Point, displays two fine Alpine-looking rock ridges, the one a series of sharp pinnacles, the other with a rounded perched block called the Helmet. *Black's Guide* described the headland as 'a striking and wonderful promontory where the Titans would seem to have been surprised by the Gods while erecting a huge palace for their king'. Beyond are the twin headlands of Carn Sperm and Carn Boel, followed by the white sands of Nanjizel (Mill Bay); this point can also be reached by a private road from Poljigga. A disintegrating pinnacle, called the Diamond Horse, looks down on the west shores of the Bay. On the far side Carn Lês Boel is pierced by a vertical slit cavern—Zawn Pyg, 'the Song of the Sea'—and ends in a steep-sided rocky promontory where there is rock climbing. Offshore is Bosistow Island.

Next we reach the wide cove of Pendower walled in opposite by Carn Barra (or Ardensaweth Cliff). Folly Cove beyond has a steep wall of rock, known as Fox Promontory, running out at right angles to the cliff; after Pellitras Point and Port Loe (which has beach pinnacles) rises the huge headland of Tol Pedn Penwith, 'the holed headland' named for the big funnel hole which goes down from cliff top to sea level on the far side. The granite 'jointed like so many blocks of Cyclopean masonry . . . is tinted all hues by weathering and by lichens, from black and grey to green, red, and a vivid orange'. There are five great rock buttresses, the most prominent being Chair Ladder below the coastguard lookout which is well seen from this side. Passing over the headland we find it possible to descend almost to sea level by the Funnel Hole and look back from there on this truly magnificent rock scenery. On the cliff above are two daymarks which are lined up on the Runnel Stone, a reef a mile offshore. Beyond the reef in the same line is the Runnel Stone Buoy which moans eerily in the wind.

Round the corner now is Porthgwarra, a small fishing village with a little sand, and tunnels through the cliff. This can be reached by road from Poljigga. The Path leads on over cliffs which are lower and less impressive, past St Levan Church and above the cove of Porth Chapel, to the headland of Pedn-mên-an-mere, looking down on the sands of Porthcurno. On the slopes of the cliff is the Minack open-air theatre, readily accessible from the Porthcurno-St Levan road; it is a fine natural amphitheatre with tiers of grass seats and an earthen stage with Grecian pillars. Porthcurno, accessible by minor road from B3315, is an important cable terminal. The remarkable shell-sand beach is said to be haunted by a spectral sailing vessel, black and square-rigged, which passes without shock from sea to land and disappears in a smoke wreath up the valley. 'Under bright sunshine', says the *Thorough Guide*, 'the lover of the sea will pause to note how, as the long ground-swell rolls in majestically, the crest as it breaks shows carnelian and topaz tints of exquisite delicacy, and then runs over the sands in creamy foam.' Nowadays on such a popular beach the transistor radio detracts substantially from similar flights of fancy, even though the sea itself has not changed.

At low water the sands are continuous as far as the Treryn Dinas peninsula. The Path continues along the cliff top, though halfway along there is access to the beach of Pedn y Vounder by a very steep path. Treryn Dinas is National Trust and is visited by numbers of people who walk across Treen Cliff from a car park at Treen. Here is perhaps the most famous of the logan (or rocking) stones; tipped over by an irresponsible Naval party in 1824, it was subsequently replaced under Admiralty orders by the officer-in-charge at his personal expense. It is said to rock even today. There are signs of an ancient camp on the promontory. The highest point of the headland, called Castle Peak, can be climbed says the *Thorough Guide* 'by those who are cragsmen'. The Path continues easily into Penberth Cove. These first six or so miles from Land's End have been straightforward going on fairly open cliff tops; henceforward the scenery is less impressive and the path a good deal less used, yet in these south-facing valleys the vegetation grows in conditions which are almost sub-tropical.

Three and a half miles of this changed coastal scenery separate Penberth and Lamorna Cove, to both of which there is access by public road. We pass Porthguarnon, with granite rocks, the woods of Boskenna, St Loy Cove (said to be one of the warmest spots in England), Boscawen Point, Tater Dû, with a greenstone climbers' crag and an automatic lighthouse (1965), and so reach Lamorna Cove, once a little port for shipping the local granite, more recently an artists' colony. Another two miles and we reach the end, for a time, of the Path. Here now is:

MOUSEHOLE (SW4626). Access by the coast road from Penzance. Frequent bus service connects with the nearest station, Penzance ($3\frac{1}{2}$m). E.C. Weds.
See: harbour; Mousehole Cave.

Offshore is St. Clement's Isle. The coast road runs along the shores of Mount's Bay, dominated by St Michael's Mount on the far side, past the lifeboat station on Penlee Point and the greenstone Penlee Quarries to Newlyn.

NEWLYN (SW4628). Contiguous with Penzance.
Modern fishing port and harbour. *See*: Art Gallery.
PENZANCE (SW46/4729). On A30. BR main line terminus.

Steamer and helicopter service to the Isles of Scilly. Youth
Hostel. E.C. Fri.
Modern resort with sands in and around. Modern small port with
some industrial activity. *See*: Museum and Library of the Royal
Geological Society of Cornwall; Morrab Gardens; Penzance
Library; Penlee Museum; the harbour and Trinity House Depot;
Parish Church. *Visit*: Newlyn; Marazion Beach; St Michael's
Mount; Isles of Scilly.

The Path resumes immediately east of the railway station, on the
road at first but soon crossing the railway on to the sands. The
beach between here and Marazion has been a particularly prolific
source of pebbles and semi-precious stones. St Michael's Mount, a
conical granite hill surmounted by a modernised castle, is connected
to the shore by a causeway which is exposed at low water. There
is a small harbour dating from the fifteenth century and a few
cottages. It is probable that this was Ictis of Diodorus Siculus,
from which the tin from the Cassiterides was shipped to the Med-
iterranean. Relics of Roman times have been found here. Later,
before the castle was built, there was a Benedictine priory (twelfth-
fifteenth century)—an appanage of the greater priory similarly sited
on Mont St Michel in Normandy.

   Ahead the coast is lower and the cliffs of easier slope. Beyond
Perranuthnoe we reach Perran Sands, then the outjutting Cudden
Point with Pixies Cove (several caves), Bessie's Cove, and Prussia
Cove, the last two notorious smugglers' sites. A mile to the east,
past Hoe Point cleft by chasms, is the long stretch of Prah Sands
with, at the far end, the last of the granite headlands, Rinsey and
Trewavas. The granite engine houses at the cliff's edge rival Botallack for situation, and here too the workings went out beneath
the sea. Rinsey Head is now National Trust.

Bibliography
O.S. 1 inch Map Sheet 189 (Land's End)
O.S. 2½ inch Map Sheets SW32, 42, 43, 53, 52
Town Guide from Penzance
Blight J. T., *A Week at the Land's End*, 1871
Hudson W. H., *The Land's End*, 1908
Rees E. A., *Old Penzance*, 1956
Nos. 4, 6, 9, 20, 22, 28, 39, 46, 47, 48, from the General
   Bibliography

Page 89 Mevagissey, Cornwall (looking NE). The village and harbour close at hand are separated from Pentewan Sands by Penare Point. Black Head juts out into St Austell Bay, with the 'Cornish Alps' once again in the distant view.

Page 90 Portwrinkle, Cornwall (looking W). Looking along Battern Cliffs towards Looe

11

TREWAVAS HEAD TO BLACK HEAD
Porthleven - Loe Bar - Mullion - Lizard Point - Cadgwith

THIS section offers attractive scenery in some striking rock types which we have not met so far—schists, serpentine, and gabbro, the geomorphological curiosity of Loe Bar and England's southerly 'land's End'—Lizard Point. It is all included in the Cornwall Area of Outstanding Natural Beauty. Here on the Lizard peninsula the National Trust is particularly well represented by the cliffs between Church and Poldhu Coves, the Marconi Memorial by Poldhu Point, sites at Polurrian Cove, Mullion Cove and Island, headlands off Predannack Wartha, Predannack Head and the coast to its south, Kynance Cove and Lizard Downs, Bass Point, the cliffs round the Devil's Frying Pan at Cadgwith and Beagles Point, one mile short of Black Head.

Serpentine, which is found in a range of shades of mottled green and red, is the basis of a local industry producing ash-trays, ornaments, etc. It outcrops at the coast between Coverack and Church Cove, Landewednack and for most of the way between Kynance and Mullion. The schists make fine cliffs round the tip of the peninsula, at Predannack Head and again north of Mullion. Carrick Luz is a dyke of gabbro. North of Gunwalloe the coastal rocks are of the killas which we have met elsewhere on our travels.

Apart from one or two shafts by Porthleven there is no mining here and, though the prospects look good, there is as yet no climbing here either. The peninsula is however fine cliff-top walking country and with one or two trifling exceptions the going is straightforward and the path easy to follow.

By the Path it is 3 miles from Trewavas to Porthleven, Porthleven to Mullion is 7 miles, Mullion to Lizard Point (Polpeor Cove) is 6 miles and Lizard to Black Head 7 miles—a total of 23 miles.

Three miles of coastline having no very special interest lead to:

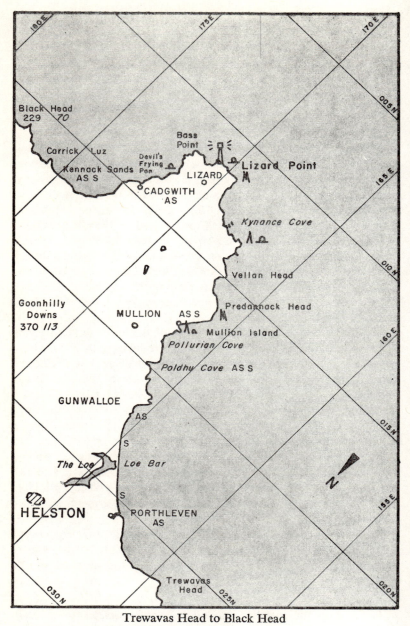

Black Head
229 *70*

Carrick Luz

Kennack Sands
AS S

Devil's
Frying
Pan

Bass
Point

LIZARD

Lizard Point

CADGWITH
AS

Kynance Cove

Vellan Head

Predannack Head

Goonhilly
Downs
370 *113*

MULLION AS S

Mullion Island

Pollurian Cove

Poldhu Cove AS S

GUNWALLOE

AS

S

The Loe

Loe Bar

N

S

HELSTON

PORTHLEVEN
AS

Trewavas
Head

Trewavas Head to Black Head

PORTHLEVEN (SW62/6325) Accessible by B3304 and B3305 from A394 by Helston. Nearest stations—Redruth (13¼m), Camborne (12½m) both with scheduled bus services to Helston. E.C. Weds. A busy fishing port.

The Path follows a trackway along Parc-an-als Cliff above the sands of Porthleven. One or two ancient mine relics are passed and then we descend to the shingle of Loe Bar, which separates the Loe, the largest natural lake in the West Country, from the sea. This is the second large shingle feature of our journey, to be compared with the Popple at Westward Ho!, but overshadowed by the mighty Chesil Beach in Dorset, which we shall reach in due course (Chapters 20 and 21). Loe Bar is a quarter of a mile long, about six hundred feet wide and mainly flint shingle; the exact process of formation is not clearly understood but it seems to have been there at least since the fourteenth century. It is conjectured that shingle spits grew from either side—from the west by tidal action; from the east by strong south-easterly winds; the final closure may have been caused by unusual tide conditions, a 'tidal wave' or tsunami. Cuts have had to be made through the Bar to prevent flooding in the lower parts of Helston, but eventually an overflow channel was made so that the lake can now be regulated. This inland water, about a mile and a quarter long with wooded banks, is an asset to the scenic amenities of the coastline.

The Path continues along the edge of a low cliff with a shingle beach below to Gunwalloe Fishing Cove, one and a quarter miles from Loe Bar; then on round Halsferran Cliff to Church Cove. The church, which nestles under the edge of the cliff called Castle Mound at the north end of the beach, dates in part from the early thirteenth century. In 1770 massive excavations were made in the sands of the cove in search of buried treasure, but nothing was found; a few years later a ship full of coins was wrecked here, but further excavations in 1845, including a dam across the cove, again failed to reward the diggers. Perhaps one should search with metal detectors? Just round the next corner is Poldhu Cove, where there is a natural arch and a large hotel. There is road access to this sandy beach from Mullion. On the cliff above, the Marconi Memorial marks the site of the eastern end of the first transatlantic wireless transmissions in 1901; twenty-two years later the first short-wave beam transmission also took place from here. Three-quarters of a mile ahead is Polurrian Cove, again with sands and a large hotel, where the schistose rocks of the Lizard begin, and beyond that Mullion Cove with tiny harbour, cave, and arch. 'Above rise on all sides', says the guidebook, 'lichen-covered cliffs, rocks piled on rocks, vaulted, tunnelled, ribbed and groined, with chasms and natural arches, like the ruins of some vast cathedral.' Mullion Island (100ft) is a quarter of a mile offshore, on the foreshore below Mullion Cliff is the conical Gull Rock (our sixth).

The Path descends to a deep gorge then climbs to the summit of Mên-te-Heul. From elevations such as this there are tremendous views across Mount's Bay to St Michael's Mount and the hills of West Penwith. The clarity or otherwise of this view is an aid to weather forecasting, for just as the inhabitants of Penzance are reported to employ 'When Lizard is clear, rain is near', so in reverse must Lizard folk derive the same information from their view of Penzance. We have now reached Predannack Head, one of the principal schistose cliffs, and quite impressive it is with ribs of rock from base to summit which have been used by rock climbers.

Soon the serpentine appears again. We pass Pol Cornick, where there is a cave called Ogodour, St George's Cove with arch and cave, and go out on to Vellan Head. Beyond in Gew-Graze Cove steatite (or soapstone) used to be quarried. Now comes what Folliott Stokes calls 'the most dramatic arrangement of crag and precipice in Cornwall'—remember too that he had walked every mile of the coast! This is an ampitheatre known as Pigeon Ogo— 'its perpendicular walls rise more than two hundred feet, and enclose in their sombre shadows a deep pool of troubled water, ever moaning and foaming in the caverns at their base . . . Beyond rises a strangely-shaped peninsula known as "The Horse". Its crest is a jagged edge of rock fangs that defy the climber, while on either side it slopes perpendicularly to the sea.' Three-quarters of a mile of cliff top brings us to Kynance, perhaps the most beautiful, certainly the best known, of Cornish Coves.

There is access by private toll road from A3083 and a car park. From the sandy beach there arises a fine assortment of cove scenery —pinnacles and islands, arches, caves, blow holes, and so forth. The largest of these is Asparagus Island with a cave, the Devil's

Throat, and two blow holes which seem to be variously named depending on the source. Beyond, and cut off always by a deep water channel, is Gull Rock (the seventh). On the beach are two pinnacles, the Sugarloaf and the Steeple, with nearby a series of caves in the main cliff—the Kitchen, the Parlour, and the Drawing Room. On the south side of the Cove the 200ft cliffs of Yellow Carn look down on another detached islet, the Lion Rock. Another half mile of up and down over high cliffs leads to Old Lizard Point, where the schistose cliffs are a possibility for the rock climber—here the coast turns abruptly eastwards. We notice here-abouts a large number of offshore reefs, reminiscent of the Pointe du Raz in Brittany, and shipping is forced well out to sea. Round the corner is Polpeor Cove with a fine cave accessible at low water. The lifeboat used to be kept here in Polbream Cove and the old lifeboat house can still be seen; nowadays it has a more sheltered east-facing site in Kilcobban Cove by Landewednack.

A lighthouse was built on Lizard as long ago as 1619 at a cost of £500; it burned coal. There were various objections, both official and by wreckers, and it was pulled down. Another was erected in 1752 and modernised in 1903 to become one of the most powerful in the world. Off the point to the east is the isolated Bumble Rock accessible at low water; between here and Pen Olver is Housel Bay with the Lions' Den funnel hole on the cliffs above. This was formed during a night in February 1847 when the roof of a sea cave called Daws Hugo collapsed. At first the sides were sheer and the bottom level and turf-covered, but the sea gradually re-moved the debris, leaving a square rocky funnel going down to sea level. Beyond Pen Olver is Belidden Cove backed by Bass Point and the Lloyd's Signal Station, which by reporting the passing of all ships contributes substantially to the national shipping intel-ligence. There is a wide bay between here and Black Head.

The Path, which in these parts is well marked and easy to follow, continues above Kilcobben Cove (lifeboat) to Landewednack Church Cove, which has been used as a tiny port, then on along the cliff edge to Cadgwith. On the way we pass another huge funnel hole, the Devil's Frying Pan, two hundred feet deep, in the lower reaches of which one can land from a boat. Indeed the boat traveller is well rewarded in this section of the cliff, for between Landewednack and Cadgwith he will see also Polbarrow

Cave, an arch beneath Carnbarrow, and Choughs' Hugo, Ravens' Hugo, and Dolor Hugo caves, the last in beautiful coloured serpentine. More than a hundred years ago Alphonse Esquiros visited Dolor Hugo during his West Country journey: 'The entrance is formed by rocks of a magnificent colour, whose arch rises to an imposing height. The entrance is at first wide enough for a six-oared boat to pass; but it soon narrows, and the end is lost in darkness. As far as the eye can penetrate, the water rises and falls with a mournful splash . . . My guide refused to go further and indeed the boat was almost squeezed by the two walls of rock. To explore the depths of the cavern, he said, would require a clever and intrepid swimmer.' Cadgwith is a famous fishing cove to which there is road access, though very little room for cars. There is a lifeboat station.

The Path makes no diversion from the sea's edge past **Polbream Point** to Kennack Sands (fine beaches). It crosses the gabbro of Carrick Luz with its earthwork, and passes on to Black Head, which at 229ft is the most outstanding cliff on this side of Lizard.

Bibliography

O.S. 1 inch Map Sheet 189 (Land's End) and 190 (Truro and Falmouth)
O.S. 2½ inch Map Sheets SW62, 61, 71
Town Guide from Helston (covers Lizard)
Cummings, A. H., *The Church and Antiquities of Cury and Gunwalloe*, 1895
Harvey, E. G., *Mullyon*, 1875
Johns, C. A., *A Week at the Lizard*, 1848
Nos. 4, 6, 9, 20, 22, 28, 39, 43, 46, 47, 48 from the General Bibliography

12

BLACK HEAD TO NARE HEAD
Coverack - Helford River - Rosemullion Head - Falmouth
St Mawes - St Anthony Head - Porthscatho - Gerrans Bay

THIS section is broken up by the arms of the Fal Estuary, so that three ferry crossings have to be made in the course of twenty-seven miles of walking. Falmouth to St Mawes is a steamer service running to timetable, the Helford River ferry is available as required during a limited period in the middle of the day, the third ferry from St Mawes to Place is not a scheduled service and cannot be relied on. Travelling in this direction there need be no difficulty; one can go round on the road to Gerrans and rejoin the Path at Porthscatho; the traveller from east to west, not wishing to miss the Roseland peninsula, may find himself trapped at Place with no obvious future to his journey.

Except for the urban area of Falmouth all this coastline is in the Cornwall Area of Outstanding Natural Beauty. Geologically it is complex. After serpentine from Black Head to Coverack and gabbro on to Porthoustock, the remainder is a complicated out-cropping of various slate beds. Finally, Nare Head at the far end is igneous pillow lava as at Pentire on the North Coast. The National Trust has a considerable holding; Lowland Point by Coverack, a fine collection of small properties round the Helford River including Rosemullion Head, farms and foreshore adding up to above half of the Roseland peninsula, including St Anthony Head and holdings on the Channel coast, Pendower Beach south-west of Veryan and Nare Head. The castles at Pendennis Point and St Mawes are in the charge of the Ministry of Public Building and Works.

The scenery in this section is quieter and more civilised than that of the north or west of Cornwall. Steers thinks the eastern coast of Lizard more attractive than the west, where the 'very flat, barren, windswept plateau is so pronounced that although it cannot spoil the actual coast it does perhaps detract from its setting. On the east the cliff scenery is far less imposing, but the many

97

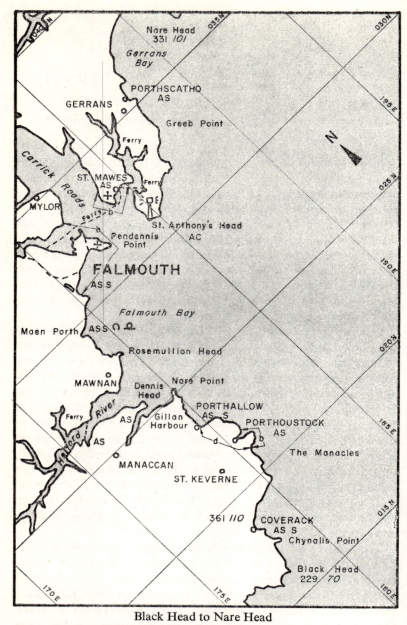

Black Head to Nare Head

(Based upon the Ordnance Survey Map, with the sanction of the Controller of HM Stationery Office, Crown Copyright reserved)

deep valleys, the woods and the less emphatic nature of the plateau all combine to give a calmer and more restful landscape.' Apart from the igneous crag of Nare Head, the cliffs are altogether less striking and of gentler slope and outline. As yet there is nothing anywhere for the rock climber.

By the Path Black Head to Porthoustock is 4½ miles and thence on to Helford River a further 6 miles. The ferry crossing is about 500yd. Helford River to Falmouth by the roundabout route of the Path is 8 miles. The ferry crossings here are of 2 miles and 1,000yd respectively. Finally Place Manor to Nare Head by the Path is 8 miles—a total walking distance of 26½ miles.

From Black Head we continue northwards, hugging as usual the cliff edge. In half a mile we reach Chynhalls Point, which Hockin described as 'once cliff-castled and now hotel-owned'. The Path goes out to the end of this curious promontory and back again, but it is easily possible to take a short cut across the base. Now down a long hill to:

COVERACK (SW7818) Accessible from Helston by B3293 and B3294. E.C. Sat.
Fishing village with small harbour and lifeboat; shingle beach.

At first the Path traverses a moorland hillside with some large ivy-covered boulders, then the hill recedes and we continue almost at sea level. Lowland Point, a curiously flat area, is a portion of raised beach dating from the Ice Age. In another mile comes Manacle Point with, offshore, the dreaded Manacles, scene of many a shipwreck. They are marked by bell buoy and light. A mile and a half inland St Keverne Church with a sixty-foot tower surmounted by a thirty-eight foot spire is a daymark which also helps the passing navigator to avoid these rocks. The Path turns inland before reaching the Point and runs across its base through Rosenithon to Porthoustock, at one time a pleasant typically Cornish cove, now devastated by huge quarry workings on the headlands on either side. The Path goes direct by track and minor road to Porthallow, a tiny fishing village at the end of a wooded valley.

Between this point and the Helford River there lies a tiny piece of unspoilt country far off the usual tourist routes, not in any way wild or rugged but soft and extremely pleasant. One mile north is Nare Point, the southern headland of the Helford River, commanding an extensive view to Rosemullion Head, the channels of the Fal River and across Falmouth Bay to Dodman Point and beyond. The Path hugs the south shore of Gillan Harbour, which is crossed either by ferry to St Anthony, by ford a little higher, or by the bridge up-river at Carne. It returns by the north shore to make a circuit of Dennis Head (fortified and captured during the Civil War) and then runs westwards near the south bank of the Helford River to Helford, a tiny village and harbour, Manaccan, three-quarters of a mile inland, which was named originally for a monk 'Manassus' who lived there, subsequently gave its name to a mineral, manaccanite, an ore of the metal titanium. We attract the attention of the ferryman and are carried over to the Ferry Boat Inn at Helford Passage.

The Path turns along the north shore and runs past Durgan and below Mawnan; a climb over Rosemullion Head leads in another mile to the little sandy beach of Maen Porth where there are caves and arches. The paths become the beaten tracks of the urban area of a resort. We cross Pennance Point and go by Swanpool to the south-facing front of Falmouth. We can encircle the famous viewpoint of Pendennis Point, on which a Henry VIII castle is sited, or we can cut straight across to the harbour area.

FALMOUTH (SW8032 and surrounding squares). Access by A39 from Truro, A393 from Redruth, A394 from Helston and BR branch line from Truro. Youth Hostel. E.C. Weds.
Called by Leland 'the principal haven of all Britain', began to grow as a port in the early seventeenth century and increased in importance throughout the days of sail. Mail Packet Station from 1688 to mid-nineteenth century when the advent of steam saw the transfer of this service to Southampton. At this time began to develop as a resort; the railway arrived in 1863. Has nevertheless always been an important cargo port and played an important role in wars, particularly the last. The harbours are on the north side of Pendennis Point facing north, the beaches are on its south side facing south. These are sandy: Castle

Beach, Gyllyngvase Beach and Swanpool. *See*: Parish Church; docks and harbour; Pendennis Castle (viewpoint). *Visit*: Places on the River Fal and its tributaries.

The wide stretch of river above Falmouth is known as Carrick Roads; the peninsula to the east is Roseland, a splendid tract of quiet, unspoilt country. We cross on the ferry to:

ST MAWES (SW8433). Access by A3078 from St Austell. Nearest stations—Falmouth (2m by ferry), Truro (19m). E.C. Thurs. Small harbour with houses in terraces above. Delightful small resort with boating. *See*: Castle.

We now seek the unscheduled and infrequent ferry across to the other side of the Porth Cuel River, to Place Manor Hotel. This is near the tip of the eastern half of the peninsula and is approached by a very minor road from Gerrans. St Anthony Church nearby dates from the thirteenth century. The Path conscientiously circumambulates Zone (or Zoze) Point to the south. On St Anthony Head is a lighthouse (1835) which is sectored white and red, the red marking a line to the Manacles and thus completing the warning system for those famous reefs by Porthoustock. There are fine views over the teeming ship life of the Bay.

We now have a wide coastal view from Manacle Point to the south-west to Nare Head and Dodman Point in the north-east and perhaps a glimpse of far-off Rame Head, or even of Dartmoor, in the distance. There is a bathing beach north of the lighthouse. The Path now takes us along the Channel coast towards Porthscatho, passing the beaches of Porthbeor below Behortha and Towan below Porth Farm. Here the Rosteague Creek all but cuts the peninsula in half. The cliffs are sloping and the adjacent land low and cultivated. Porthscatho, a small fishing village, lies in a low bay and not in the usual steep cove. The parish church inland at Gerrans has a tall spire used as a daymark. Hereabouts the traveller by the road route from St Mawes will rejoin the Path.

Two miles of undistinguished walking at the cliff edge lead on to Pendower Beach, a considerable stretch of sand. Thenceforward the Path is easy to follow out to the fine rocky Nare Head. At Pradda Cove is an arch called Fregeagh's Cave. The Head reaches 331ft and 'its cliffs bristle with slatey fangs'; it just about misses being a climbing site. Gull Rock (the eighth), 125ft high and half a mile offshore is said, when reached by boat, to offer scrambling on arêtes and pinnacles, also a cavern. Some of the rock outlines look almost Alpine. This and Middle and Outer Stones mark one of the rare outcrops of igneous rocks on this southern Cornwall coast.

Bibliography

O.S. 1 inch Map Sheet 190 (Truro and Falmouth)
O.S. 2½ inch Map Sheets SW71, 72, 73, 83
Town Guide from Falmouth
Gray, S. E., *Old Falmouth*, 1903
Nos. 4, 6, 9, 20, 22, 28, 39, 43, 47, 48 from the General Bibliography

13

NARE HEAD TO FOWEY

Portloe - Portholland - Dodman Point - Gorran Haven
Mevagissey - Black Head - Charlestown - Par
Gribbin Head - Fowey

IN this section we can contrast some of the loveliest scenery in South Cornwall with the industrial devastation of the coastline at Par. The latter is excluded for obvious reasons from the Cornwall Area of Outstanding Natural Beauty; the remainder is all included. The National Trust holdings include Jacka Point south-west of Portloe, Hemmick Beach and Dodman Point, Bodrugan's Leap by Chapel Point and five miles of coastline round Gribbin Head. The rocks are mainly slates; Dodman Point curiously enough is a grey slate not particularly resistant, so that it is surprising to find that it has survived as such a prominent and protruding headland. Many of the headlands are igneous rocks: Nare Head (as we have already seen), The Blouth, Jacka Point, Hartriza Point and Caragloose Point. Greeb Point is volcanic ash, Black Head on the north of Mevagissey Bay is greenstone. A mile or two inland from St Austell Bay is the great china-clay producing district round the borders of the granite mass of Hensbarrow Down. East of Par the headlands, including the imposing Gribbin Head, mark the occurrence of more resistant bands in the rocks.

In the middle of the eighteenth-century a search was made in Europe for the raw materials used to make porcelain in China— petuntse and kaolin. These are both products of altered granite and in 1755 William Cooksworthy discovered deposits at Tre- gonning near Helston. These were limited in extent, but soon after- wards extensive finds were made around Hensbarrow Downs, and St Austell grew up in the centre of the industry. The rock is ex- tracted from huge pits sometimes 300ft deep and half a mile across; only a percentage of the material thus obtained is china-clay, the remainder is piled in huge white heaps hundreds of feet high on which no vegetation will grow, so that they loom up in the land- scape like snow mountains. The Cornish Alps, as they are often

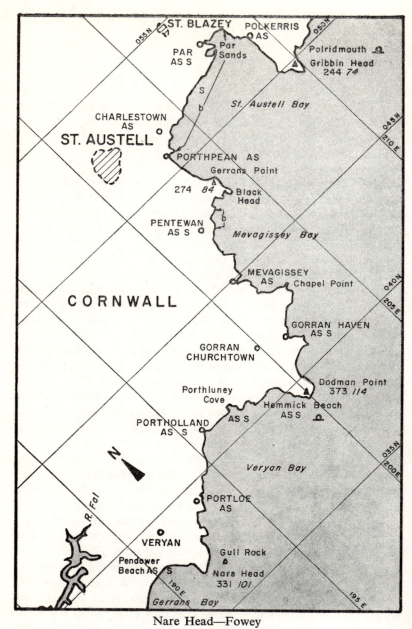

Nare Head—Fowey

called, form a startling backdrop to many of the views in this section of the coastline.

By the Path, Nare Head to Dodman Point is 8 miles, Dodman Point to Mevagissey 5½ miles, Mevagissey to Charlestown 7 miles, Charlestown to Par (which should be avoided or done at night or with the eyes shut) 3½ miles and Par to Fowey 6 miles—a total of 30 miles.

There is fine elevated walking on the plateau top of Nare Head with rocks which do not quite reach the status of climbable on the seaward slopes. Passing the rocky Kilberick Cove, The Blouth and Manare Point we come in two miles to the small fishing village of Portloe. When Folliott Stokes came here more than sixty years ago his visit coincided with the weekly bus, actually 'twice a week to Truro and once to St Austell'; it was a rickety old wagonette drawn by 'a most antiquated-looking steed . . . packed with villagers all in their Sunday best'. What a difference the car has made for us! The Path continues to hug the sea's edge for another two miles to West Portholland, which is connected by a short length of cart-track with East Portholland; both have small beaches, a few cottages and road access. It is a straightforward cliff path to a point just above Porthluney and we walk down a short length of road into the Cove (road access and beach).

Behind rises the imposing mass of Caerhayes Castle, John Nash 'Gothick' dating from 1808, which replaced an ancient castle on the same site. The huge promontory of Dodman Point, projecting almost a mile in front of the main coastline, which has been filling the view for some time, now looms only a mile or so ahead. The Path continues past Greeb Point to Hemmick Beach (sands, caves, and motorable track access from Boswinger—camp site and Youth Hostel) immediately against the base of the Point. The whole headland is National Trust; signposted footpaths lead out to the end, which is 373ft. Here there is a tall granite cross, erected by a former vicar of St Michael Caerhays, which now serves as a daymark. The view is far-reaching—along the coast from Black Head on Lizard to Bolt Head in Devonshire, Eddystone Light-house, the Cornish Alps around Hensbarrow Downs, Brown Willy and the other hills of Bodmin Moor and Caradon Hill with its TV mast. There are remains of former earthworks of uncertain date across the base of the headland; we cross these and continue our way along the coast eastwards towards Gorran Haven. This is sheltered on the south by a smooth conical hill of 280ft. There is a sandy beach with a quay, divided by an arm of the cliff, and road access from Gorran Churchtown. Gwineas Rocks a mile off-shore are marked by a bell buoy. The Path continues along the cliff, passing a small rock pinnacle on Pabyer Point, and rounds Chapel Point to the road again at Port Mellon. On the way we pass the site of Bodrugan's Leap, where, after the Battle of Bosworth in 1485, Sir Henry Trenowth of Bodrugan pursued by Sir Richard Edgcumbe of Cotehele leaped on his horse over (or down) the cliff to a boat waiting to take him to France. As consolation Edgcumbe received Trenowth's lands and his castle, half a mile inland, now sadly only a farm. From Port Mellon a road leads round Stuckumb Point to:

MEVAGISSEY (SX0144). Access by B3273 from St Austell. Nearest station—St Austell (6m). E.C. Thurs.
Once just another fishing village with narrow streets and two harbours, where Folliott Stokes noted 'appalling smells'. Now a popular small resort with sand and shingle beach. *See*: Church; aquarium.

Beyond the Coast Guard Station is Polstreath Beach; the Path skirts this and, rounding Penare Point, joins the road again near Pentewan Beach. There is a large caravan site and our route is forced to follow the road behind it to the bridge over the St Austell River. This has been polluted for a very long time—once by tin streaming and by adits from mines like Polgooth three miles upstream, where at one time there were twenty-six shafts simultaneously in operation, later by white discharge from china-clay workings. Tin working near the river mouth, says Salmon, was 'carried on at some depth below sea level and there were found the horns of Irish elk, not petrified, but completely metallised by the tin ore'. Hastening past this over-civilised corner, we find our selves almost immediately on a very quiet piece of coast indeed, which brings us in a mile and a half to the projecting Black Head, with cliff camp, now protected by National Trust covenants. On the way is Hallane beach reached by a steep pedestrian track down

Page 107 Start Point, South Devon (looking WNW). Looking from the lighthouse straight along the backbone of the ridge. Further left are Peartree Point, Matchcombe and Lannacombe and the raised beach running towards Prawle Point, backed by an ancient cliff line

Page 108 Berry Head, South Devon (looking W). Quarries and climbers' crags in Devonian limestone. Beyond lie Brixham and its harbour and the beginnings of the sweep of Tor Bay

a narrow valley from Trenarren. Beyond is Gerrans Point. 'In the cliffes between the Blak-Hed and Tywartraith Bay', says Leland, 'is a certeyn cave, wheryn apperith thinges lyke images giltid, and also in the same cliffes be vaynes of metalles, as coper and other.' Another mile and we reach the road again at Porthpean, where there is a sandy beach. St Austell is only a mile and a half away, so this is a popular spot for visitors. Now there is a straightforward path by way of Duporth (large holiday camp) to Charlestown.

Charlestown is a tiny active port mainly used for china-clay traffic. There are lock gates to keep the ships afloat at low tide and, though it is probably not allowed, the traveller may sometimes cross these gates to get past more quickly. Folliott Stokes found it 'a Gehenna—on one side of the harbour vessels were being loaded with china clay, and their crews were as white as millers. On the other side coal was being discharged, and here the crews were as black as Erebus. The villagers were black or white, according to which side they resided on. While some were both black and white.' He wrongly ascribed its name to King Charles I; in fact it is named for Charles Rashleigh, who was responsible for the construction of the port in the late eighteenth century.

There are some dull miles ahead for the traveller who enjoys unspoilt coastline and, if it were possible to sail over the Bay and rejoin the Path at Polkerris, this would certainly be a recommended course. Uphill from Charlestown and we find a cliff top covered with large houses and hotels—Carlyon Bay; threading them we pass above the sandy Crinnis Beach and round the corner to Par Harbour. This is a modern and of course a much bigger and much improved version of what Folliott Stokes found at Charlestown. The river once flowed to St Blazey Bridge but was gradually silted up by the debris from tin streaming.

PAR (SX0753). On A3082 just off A380 and on BR Main Line. E.C. Thurs. Youth Hostel at Lostwithiel (5m).
Sands, caravans and other resort amenities. Surroundings heavily industrialised. *Visit*: Luxulyan Valley (2m).

The main road cuts across the base of the next peninsula, Gribbin Head, while the Path takes a lengthy and scenic circuit of the

G

cliff's edge. Now we are back on worthwhile going once again. In
a mile comes the pleasant sandy cove of Polkerris, where there is a
small stone pier. Gribbin Head jutting aggressively southwards is
244ft high and surmounted by an 84ft shipping landmark, erected by
Trinity House in the 1830s. The view extends from Dodman Point
on the one hand to Rame Head and beyond on the other. Close
at hand round the corner is Pridmouth Cove, with a sandy beach
and 'almost sub-tropical flora'; there is a grotto, interior walls
and roof covered with minerals, crystals, agates, and so on. The
Path continues to St Catherine's Castle, built by King Henry VIII,
of which but little remains. Nearby is the curious Rashleigh
Mausoleum and there is a fine view out over Fowey Harbour. Down
below on either side of the water are two stone block-houses; a
chain between them was used to close the Harbour in mediaeval
times when raiders were sighted. From Readymoney Cove there is
a road into Fowey.

FOWEY (SX1251/52). Access by A3082. Nearest stations—Par
(4m), St Austell (9m). Ferries from Polruan and Bodinnick. Youth
Hostel at Golant (2m). E.C. Weds.
Ancient port of great importance in mediaeval times, sending
47 ships to Edward III's siege of Calais, the largest number from
any port in England. Now a popular resort and yachting centre,
with china-clay export wharves up river. The only sand is at
Readymoney Cove, but there are notable numbers of boat trips
available in every direction. *See*: Parish Church; St Catherine's
Castle. *Visit*: Hall Walk (above Bodinnick); by boat (in the
harbour) Pont Pill; Lerryn River; Penpoll Creek (outside it) the
adjacent towns and villages up and down the coast.

Bibliography

O.S. 1 inch Map Sheets 190 (Truro and Falmouth), 186 (Bodmin
and Launceston)
O.S. 2½ inch Maps Sheets SW83, 94, SX04, 05, 15
Town Guides from St Austell and Fowey
Keast, J., *The Story of Fowey*, 1950
Shore, Commander H. N., *Smugglers of Fowey* (F. Graham, New-
castle, 1964)
Nos. 4, 6, 9, 20, 22, 28, 39, 43, 47, 48 from the General Bibliography

14

FOWEY TO PORTWRINKLE

Polruan - Polperro - Looe - Seaton - Downderry

RICHARD CAREW in his *Survey of Cornwall* wrote thus of the coast immediately east of Fowey: 'In passing along your eyes shall be called away from guiding your feet, to descry by their farthest kenning the vast ocean sprinkled with ships that continually this way trade forth and back to most quarters of the world. Nearer home, they take view of all sized cocks, barges and fisherboats, hovering on the coast. Again, contracting your sight to a narrower scope, it lighteth on the fair and commodious haven, where the tide daily presenteth his double service of flowing and ebbing, to carry and recarry whatsoever the inhabitants shall be pleased to charge him withal, and his creeks (like a young wanton lover) fold about the land with many embracing arms.'

From Fowey River to within a mile or so of West Looe we travel once again in the Cornwall Area of Outstanding Natural Beauty. The National Trust is, as usual, well represented with St Saviour's Point above Fowey Harbour mouth, an extensive holding stretching from Blackbottle Point round Lantic Bay to Pencarrow Head including parts of Lantivet Bay and notably that part below Lansallos, one mile of coast west of Polperro and Bodigga Cliff and foreshore beside Millendraeth Beach. The first part of this section is pleasant enough, while the path from Polperro to Looe is well-maintained and easy to follow; east of Looe the influence of Plymouth begins to obtrude and there are caravan sites, shacks, new building and so on to detract from the scenery. There is frequent road access to sea and cliff edge.

The rocks are mainly Dartmouth Slates, which, says Steers, 'often show bright colours, especially in Talland Bay where Indian red and green tints predominate. Green colours are very striking near Sharrow Point.'

The ferry crossing from Fowey to Polruan is about 600yd; thence by the Path, Polruan to Polperro is $7\frac{1}{2}$ miles, Polperro to Looe is 5 miles and Looe to Portwrinkle 8 miles—a total of $20\frac{1}{2}$ miles.

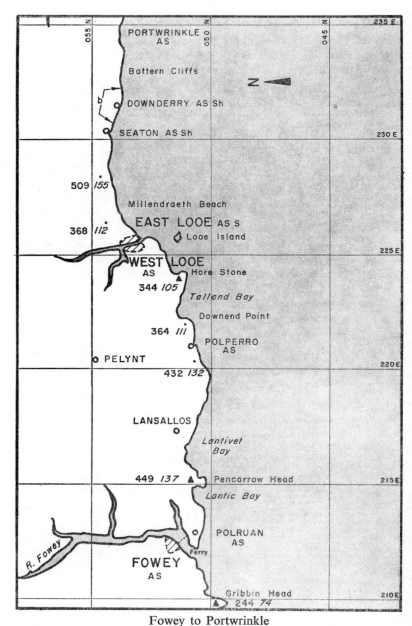

Fowey to Portwrinkle

(Based upon the Ordnance Survey Map, with the sanction of the Controller of HM Stationery Office, Crown Copyright reserved)

There is a frequent ferry service from Fowey to Polruan, running for reasonably long hours. This is a busy harbour with yachts, and steamers up to 10,000 tons carrying china clay. The steep main street climbs directly from the harbour but the Path skirts the shore, passing the site of this end of the defensive boom, and so to the National Trust land of St Saviour's Head. Now once again we open out a wide view of the English Channel. In a mile comes the steep Blackbottle Point, almost reaching 400ft, the western headland of Lantic Bay. There is a tremendous view from Dodman Point to Rame Head, Gribbin Head with its daymark and the moors and 'Alps' of Hensbarrow beyond.

On the far side of the Bay is Pencarrow Head, to which there is access by footpath from the road out of Polruan. The hill above the headland is 449ft. Lantivet Bay is wide with a number of pleasant sandy coves backed by easy cliffs. There was once a quay in Palace Cove. There is footpath access from the road here also. A bell buoy offshore and a white-washed beacon onshore mark the position of the dangerous Udder Rock. Below the village of Lansallos is Lansallos Head (National Trust) which is 450ft close to the cliff edge; immediately beyond we have to descend almost to sea level where a valley comes down from Polventen. A slightly curved coastline of sloping cliffs leads round to the start of the Polperro National Trust area. A well preserved stretch of sloping cliff, with fine paths and shelters, below Hard Head (432ft) leads in just over a mile to:

POLPERRO (SX20/2150). Access by A387 from West Looe. Nearest station—Looe ($4\frac{1}{2}$m). E.C. Sat.
Built in a steep cleft between 400ft cliffs on either hand; the streets are narrow, the houses jumbled one above the other. Tourist-attracting activities abound, for it is a very popular place of pilgrimage. Cars are left in parks higher in the valley and the pilgrims descend on foot past all the attractions to the miniature habour, where the entrance is narrow enough to be closed by timber baulks in rough weather. It looks very different out of season when much of the original atmosphere can still be caught. It was a fishing port as long ago as the fourteenth century. There is a sand-shingle beach at low water by the pier,

sandy coves along the cliff path towards Talland and a submerged forest offshore.

The next section of the Path between here and Looe is notable for its excellent state of maintenance, and it is a joy to follow. We continue close to the cliff's edge east of Polperro, looking back first on the busy harbour, backed by the outjutting 90ft headland called 'The Peak'. Couch reports that in the great storm of 1817 'the tides swept over the highest point of the Peak, and, as near as the eye could judge at double the height of the rock, not in mere spray, but in a solid body of water'. Soon we reach Downend Point and round a corner into Talland Bay with its outcroppings of beautifully coloured slates. Between a pair of black and white beacons on the headland opposite and a similar pair on the hill above Polperro is the Admiralty 'Measured Mile' used in speed trials by ships at sea. The eastern side of the Bay terminates in Horestone Head (344ft), named, says Folliott Stokes, 'from a great vertical fang of slate that rises from the lower part of its seaward face, invisible from the summit, but a conspicuous object from the sea'. We now circle Portnadler Bay with the considerable island called St George's, or Looe Island rising to 150ft offshore. This was once a promontory and more recently was inhabited, though no longer. Eventually the Path comes out on the coast road just short of Hannafore Point and we walk on this into West Looe.

LOOE (SX2553). Access by A387 and by BR branch line from Liskeard. E.C. Thurs.

The towns of East and West Looe, which face one another across the combined East and West Looe Rivers, are joined by an ancient bridge, rebuilt in the nineteenth century. Above the bridge, each of the rivers is a pleasing and wide stretch of tidal water. The towns sent 20 ships to join Edward III at the siege of Calais; this is still an important fishing port. *See*: Old Guildhall and Museum; St Nicholas's Church; Aquarium; Banjo pier and sands; *Visit*: (on land) Devil's Hedge (earthen rampart with ditch which ran from Looe to Lerryn); (by water) places on the rivers and along the coast on either hand; Eddystone Lighthouse.

If the author of *Guide to Watering Places* had visited much of the West Country coastline he would surely have run out of superlatives, for he says of the section from Looe to Plymouth—'sea, promontories, rocks and precipices combine to form a terrible sublimity'. If only they did!

The coast path used to climb on to the cliffs from the eastern end of the beach at East Looe, but there have been cliff falls here in recent years so that the Path now runs through the town from a point close to the bridge and crosses the shoulder of the hill on to the seaward face of the cliffs. At first there are houses and bungalows, which cannot be avoided. The coast is coming now more and more under the influence of Plymouth, for which it serves as dormitory or weekend playground. We pass Plaidy Beach and in a mile of wide trackway come to Millendraeth Beach, where there are caravans and National Trust properties.

In the next two miles to Seaton the Path will continue to follow the cliff edge. There is an alternative road line close inland reached by a steep path out of Millendraeth which leads to a few hundred yards of excellent roadway, the purpose of which in such a remote spot is obscure. Folliott Stokes took to the beach for this section: '. . . level walking over sand and low rocks. Above us towered slate cliffs, often much distorted, their less precipitous slopes being a jungle of bracken, ivy-clad pinnacles and elder and fruit bushes . . .' Seaton, with caravan sites and chalets, has a sandy beach. There is road access alongside the Seaton River down the Hessenford Valley and also along the coast eastwards towards Downderry. This road is close to the sea's edge and the line of the Path, which just avoids it on the seaward side, is somewhat academic. We pass through a mile of houses, shops, etc, old and new, the Path eventually giving up trying and collapsing into the road. When this turns inland to avoid the steep slopes of Battern Cliff, the Path strikes off once again into the comparative wild, a straightforward route across vegetation covered slopes and out on to the open cliff top at over 450ft, the highest cliffs in fact on the South Cornwall coast. Soon the road (B3247) comes crowding in again, but the Path just manages to keep out of contact. We pass 'some pinasters and a bungalow (once) belonging to Lord St Germans, known as St Germans Hut' and, two miles from Downderry, reach the tiny village of Portwrinkle, once a busy smuggling centre. In this stretch too Folliott Stokes preferred to proceed by the beach. In one place he had to 'clamber over a reef of very rough rocks and for a quarter of a mile progressed by a series of acrobatic evolutions'. Then an impassable wall of rock made it necessary for him to climb up the cliff by a narrow path just short of Portwrinkle.

Bibliography

O.S. 1 inch Map Sheet 186 (Bodmin and Launceston)
O.S. 2½ inch Maps Sheets SX15, 25, 35
Town Guide from Looe
Bond, J., *East and West Looe*, 1823
Couch, Jonathan, *The History of Polperro*, 1871 (reprinted F. Graham, Newcastle, 1965)
Nos. 4, 6, 9, 20, 22, 28, 39, 43, 47, 48 from the General Bibliography

15

PORTWRINKLE TO
ST ANCHORITE'S ROCK

Whitesand Bay - Rame Head - Cawsand - Kingsand
Plymouth - Newton Ferrers - Noss Mayo

THIS section includes the great seaport of Plymouth. The Cornwall section of the Path ends at Cremyll Ferry by the Hamoaze; the Devon section starts at Turnchapel. From Rame Head to Cremyll in particular the route is well sign posted. There is nothing charming about the slopes above Whitesand Bay, which are overgrown with shacks, nor those on the sides of Plymouth Sound, where there are relics of fortification and noisy gunfire can be heard at intervals from the practice ranges.

We have left behind now the Cornwall Area of Outstanding Natural Beauty, though the correspondingly designated area of Devonshire starts at Bovisand and stays with us for many a mile thereafter. The National Trust is again well represented with Trethill Cliff, Sharrow Point and Higher Tregantle Cliffs above Whitesand Bay, Drake's Island in Plymouth Sound and a sizeable stretch of coast from Wembury along the Yealm Estuary. The coastal rocks are again almost entirely Dartmouth Slates and again notably coloured. 'Pink, purple and green in Whitesand Bay', says Trueman, while Hockin writes of 'caverned cliffs varying in colour from off-white and a bilious yellow to warm Devon red, purple and black'. The headlands such as Rame and Penlee are slates also, strengthened by bands of quartz and grit. The cliffs of Plymouth Hoe however are of Devonian limestone, while Drake's Island is granite.

By the Path, Portwrinkle to Rame Head is 6½ miles and Rame Head to Cremyll Ferry 5 miles. The ferry crossing of about 1,000yd is followed by 2 miles through urban Plymouth and a bus journey to Turnchapel. Now on the Devon section, Turnchapel to Warren Point is 7 miles, the Yealm Ferry (when in operation) is about 250yd (the detour is 10 miles) and finally Yealm Ferry to St Anchorite's Rock 7 miles—a total of 27½ miles of walking.

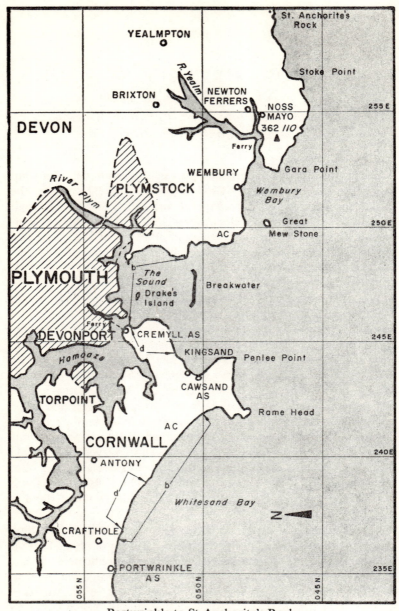

Portwrinkle to St Anchorite's Rock

(Based upon the Ordnance Survey Map, with the sanction of the Controller of HM Stationery Office, Crown Copyright reserved)

On the golf course to the east of Portwrinkle is a good example of a mediaeval pigeon-cote or culver-house. We set out once again eastwards still, remember, on the coast where 'sea, promontories, rocks and precipices combine to form a terrible sublimity'. Our civilisation knows how to tame that sort of place! After a short stretch of road at Portwrinkle Beach the Path makes off to the right for half a mile in a brave effort to be a path in truth as well as in name, but willy-nilly we are forced off to the road beyond Crafthole. There are nearly two miles of road mostly out of sight of the sea, round behind Tregantle Fort (disused) and a series of rifle ranges. There is a fine view over Plymouth and the anchorages. The cliff edge is reached again at Tregantle Down. Now it is possible, and much wiser if the tide is right, to take to the beach, here called Long Sands, though even this might be hazardous if the red flags were up for firing. All the scenery looks better from here, especially if we avoid looking at the cliffs ahead. Sharrow Point, when we reach it, has slates which are notably green.

The two-mile stretch ahead, in Harper's time 'crossing lonely down', is nowadays one of the worst parts of the whole Path. The sloping cliff front is dotted with bungalows, shacks, caravans, and so on, weekend retreats one would assume for Plymothians. The best route would be on the beach, with eyes firmly right; the road which passes through these habitations has nothing to commend it, except sometimes the view over the countryside to the north, to Kit Hill and Caradon. At the end of the sands the former Polhawn Battery is now a private residence. We follow cliff paths to the jutting promontory of Rame Head, surmounted by a one-time cliff castle and the ruins of a chapel of St Michael. There is an expansive view from Bolt Tail to the Lizard with the tall tower of Eddystone Lighthouse eight miles ahead in the sea.

Henceforward the Path is well-marked and easy to follow. In one and a half miles we reach Penlee Point, the western portal of Plymouth Sound, and in another mile along wooded slopes the twins—Cawsand and Kingsand. These are typical Cornish fishing villages with narrow winding streets, as John Betjeman has said 'singularly unartificial, an unspoiled and much smaller Polperro'. All along this section are the ancient forts which used to defend the approaches to the anchorage, while out in mid-channel the Breakwater, completed in 1841, lies athwart the stream, a mile long with a fort and lights. Mount Edgcumbe is ahead, a green conical hill on the edge of the Hamoaze, with the streets and houses of Stonehouse only a few hundred yards away on the opposite bank. It would be pleasant if the Path could traverse its edge round to the Cremyll Ferry and this may indeed happen one day. At present where the park begins at Hooe Lake Point about a mile ahead, the Path turns inland and climbs to Maker Church. There is an extensive view. We continue northwards down to the shore of Millbrook Lake and traverse the north shore of the peninsula through Empacombe to Cremyll. A small steamer takes us over to Admirals Hard at Stonehouse and into Devonshire.

This ferry has been in existence since the mid-thirteenth century and was once the main route into Cornwall, which continued along ridge lines to Looe and Fowey. In Celia Fiennes' time the crossing was by rowing boat: 'I was at least an hour in going over, about a mile, and notwithstanding there was five men rowing and I set my men to row also, I do believe we made not a step of way for almost a quarter of an hour, but blessed be God, I came safely over at last.' This was before the construction of the Breakwater.

PLYMOUTH (SXE45 to 50, N53 to 58). Major road and rail centre. Local ferry services to Cremyll and Torpoint. Youth Hostel. E.C. Weds.

The largest and most important place along the whole length of the Path, comprises the contiguous Plymouth, Devonport and Stonehouse. It is built on a broad nose of land between the Rivers Tamar and Plym. The Tamar, for most of its length the Cornwall/Devon border, rises near the north coast by Marsland Mouth and is joined by the Tavy from Dartmoor and the Lynher from South Cornwall. The anchorage, known as the Hamoaze, is the lower part of the river below the famous Brunel railway bridge and the new suspension road bridge at Saltash. The lower part of the Plym, which also flows off Dartmoor, is the Cattewater. The waters unite off Plymouth in the broad channel of the Sound where the protective Breakwater is strategically placed. There are forts on either side from Bovisand round to Tregantle.

There was a fishing village at Sutton before the Conquest and this grew under the shelter of Plympton Priory. The name

Plymouth dates from the thirteenth century when a great expedition sailed from here for France. The French attacked and burned the port in 1329, yet a few years later twenty-six ships were sent to Edward III for the siege of Calais. The Black Prince passed through on his way to Poitiers and returned this way with the captured French king. Around 1370 and again in 1403 the French sacked Plymouth, so a castle was built, still there in Leland's time. Margaret of Anjou landed here before Tewkesbury and Catherine of Aragon before Henry VIII. In Elizabethan times many of the explorers of the New World sailed from Plymouth, while every schoolchild knows of Sir Francis Drake's bowling nonchalance here in the face of the Armada. In 1617 Sir Walter Raleigh departed for South America, losing his head on return; in 1620 the *Mayflower* left for places further north. Fourteen miles offshore the Eddystone Rocks were a continuous menace to shipping; the story of the building of the lighthouse is an epic; the present tower was built by Douglass in 1882, when the earlier one by Smeaton was re-erected on The Hoe.

Slowly Plymouth developed as one of England's great naval bases, playing a major part in our naval history. In the Second World War a great deal of the city was destroyed by bombing, but this enabled a major rebuilding plan to be initiated with the splendid results we see today.

See: The Hoe with its views, statues and Smeaton's lighthouse; the Citadel; aquarium, Tamar bridges; Drake's Island. *Visit*: Mount Edgcumbe; Kingsand, Cawsand and Rame Head; St John's Lake and Torpoint wild-life site; Saltram House (N.T.) by Plympton.

We travel by bus to Turnchapel and set out along the South Devon section of the Path.

This follows the road at first past Stamford Fort, built on the site of an ancient burial ground. The Path continues to Staddon Heights, with another fort, a golf course and radio masts above, then descends to Bovisand Bay (road access), where naval ships used to come in to take water from a reservoir in the hills above. There are tremendous views over the Sound to Cornwall, but no notable cliffs. Soon we come abreast of the Shag Stone, marked by a light, and the route begins to swing away eastwards where the coastline looks out into the English Channel once again. There is road access to the cliff above. Off Wembury Point is the Great Mew Stone, 'the summit a crag as bare as a Dartmoor tor', says Page. It was inhabited at one time by a couple who farmed rabbits and fish for the owner.

The Path follows the cliff edge east for one mile to Wembury, the lonely church of which rises in National Trust land on the cliff top above Blackstone Rocks. We are now entering the estuary of the Yealm, but it is another half a mile to Warren Point where a ferry is available on demand. The detour round the headwaters of the Yealm is round 10 miles. Further up the river are:

NEWTON FERRERS and NOSS MAYO (SX5447). Facing one another across Newton Creek, joined by stepping stones at low water. Access by minor roads from A379. E.C. Thurs.

On the other side we follow the south bank of the river to Mouth-stone Point and then contour cliff slopes to Gara Point and the seaward-facing slopes once again. Two miles ahead there is a sandy cove at Stoke with footpath access from Noss Mayo, while nearby are the ruins of Revelstoke Church, the ancient parish church of Noss. A substantial trackway leads on to Beacon Hill, thereafter a cliff path again for a further two miles to St Anchorite's Rock—'a tor about thirty feet in height, upstanding suddenly from a brake of furze'. This is quiet, secluded countryside.

Bibliography

O.S. 1 inch Map Sheets 186 (Bodmin and Launceston), 187 (Plymouth)
O.S. 2½ inch Maps Sheets SX35, 45, 55, 54
Town Guide from Plymouth
Gill, C., *Plymouth: A New History*, Newton Abbot 1966
Gill, C., *Plymouth in Pictures*, Newton Abbot 1968
Grimes, G. N. D., *The Story of Newton Ferrers*, n.d.
Porter, P. E. B., *Around and about Saltash*, 1905
Walling, R. A. J., *The Story of Plymouth*, Westaway 1950
Nos. 4, 6, 9, 20, 26, 27, 37, 39, 43, 44 from the General Bibliography

16

ST ANCHORITE'S ROCK TO SLAPTON

Bigbury - Hope Cove - Bolt Tail - Bolt Head - Salcombe
Prawle Point - Start Point - Torcross - Slapton

THE cliff scenery in this section is the finest in South Devon; indeed, Burton claims that the view from Gammon Head over the National Trust lands on either side of Salcombe Harbour cannot be surpassed in either North Devon or North Cornwall. The whole length is in the South Devon Area of Outstanding Natural Beauty, while here also, between Hope Cove and Salcombe Harbour, is the longest continuous coast property owned by the National Trust, a length of six miles. Eastwards from the Harbour is another five miles of holding which includes Gammon Head and Prawle Point. The Trust also has small properties at Bigbury and Lannacombe, as well as a house, part Youth Hostel and part museum, at Sharpitor, Salcombe.

As far as Hope Cove the cliffs are slates of the Lower Devonian, Dartmouth Beds to Ringmore, and Meadfoot Beds the rest. Borough Island is a large stack of the Meadfoot Beds. From Bolt Tail round to Start Point we find highly metamorphosed schists, green schists, and mica schists often strengthened by quartz veins. Again the colours are noteworthy—pale yellow to dull green weathered in places to red and brown. The rock weathers often with curiously fretted edges, such as at Gammon Head, or into grotesque pinnacles as at Sharpitor on Bolt Head and the pinnacled arête of Start Point. There should certainly be possibilities for the rock climber here on walls and beach pinnacles, while nothing has been done so far towards the traverse of any of these cliff sections along the shore. East of Prawle Point there is a raised beach below the rocks of the old cliff line; curious earth pinnacles have been formed at Matchcombe by the erosion of this beach. Prawle is the most southerly point of Devon; at Start the coast turns north, and soon we are on Meadfoot Beds again with a continuous shingle beach subject to severe erosion. There is frequent access to the sea and cliff edge.

By the Path it is $2\frac{1}{2}$ miles from St Anchorite's Rock to Erme Mouth. The river here is a potential hold-up—it can be waded with care at low water on a falling tide; there is a second ford a mile upstream but the first bridge involves a considerable detour (to A379). From Erme Mouth it is $5\frac{1}{2}$ miles to the mouth of the River Avon, where there is a ford at low tide or an occasional ferry to Bantham (the detour is 7 miles); another 5 miles brings us to Inner Hope. Inner Hope to Splat Cove at Salcombe is $6\frac{1}{4}$ miles; it is a mile through urban Salcombe to a 200yd ferry crossing to East Portlemouth. 8 Miles of Path lead from here to Start Point and another $4\frac{1}{2}$ miles on to Slapton—a total Path length of 32 miles.

A little way beyond St Anchorite's Rock the Path is forced inland just short of Battisborough Island, which is cut off from the main cliff by a narrow channel. There is a private beach ahead at Mothecombe; the Path runs inland for three-quarters of a mile to a minor road which is followed east, south, then east again to the riverside in the estuary. We have noted the fording possibilities above; great care is needed and, where possible, local advice should be sought.

The Path resumes its journey from Wonwell Beach opposite. The cliffs are sloping at first but they soon steepen and reach over three hundred feet at Beacon Point. A mile ahead at Hoist Point there are steep crags on the seaward face which might almost serve the climber. We descend to Westcombe Beach, climb out and over and descend again to Ayrmer Cove. There are sands here with beach pinnacles and so forth which might give climbing. Up and over again leads to Challaborough, an extensive caravan town from which we escape with all haste round the next corner to Bigbury-on-Sea (Youth Hostel).

This coast must have been wild and remote at the end of last century when Page could write: 'Bigbury Bay is a lonesome place . . . and is likely to remain lonesome to the end . . . The district has probably altered little in the last hundred years, nor is the next century likely to effect much of a change.' With numerous access roads (nine in the next $4\frac{1}{2}$ miles between here and

Page 125 Ladram Bay and High Peak, East Devon (looking W). Ladram Bay and its pinnacles in pre-caravan days and the high red cliffs of High Peak. In the background across the River Exe are Dawlish Warren and Starcross

Page 126 East Cliff and West Bay, Dorset (looking NW). The horizontally stratified cliffs are orange-yellow. West Bay has a prominent caravan park and a small harbour, entirely artificial, at the mouth of the River Brit

Hope Cove) leading to an extensive stretch of beaches, the car has taken care of the lonesomeness and this can no longer be numbered among the wilder and less crowded sections. Offshore is Borough (or Burgh) Island (161ft) surmounted by a large hotel. This is accessible across the sands at low tide, and at other times stilted tracked vehicles serve for the sea crossing. After a short stretch of road the Path follows the north bank of the River Avon until we arrive opposite Bantham. The river can be waded at low water— the ford may be marked one day by a line of buoys. It is 7 miles round it on the land.

Returning along the south bank of the river we soon find ourselves above the sea once again; here are Thurlestone Golf Links. The inland view embraces some large hotels; seawards are sands and sands. Bolt Tail looms ahead with Hope Cove by its base. Nearer at hand on the foreshore is the isolated sandstone arch known as the Thurlestone Rock, for which the surroundings are named. In a storm it roars, says an early writer, with 'a trumpet-like sound that can be heard as far away as Kingsbridge, four miles away'. There are beach pinnacles and possible climbs by Hope Cove.

HOPE (SX6739/40). Access by minor road from Malborough on A381. Nearest station—Totnes (19m).
Small fishing village famous for crabs, now small resort with sandy beach and fine cliff scenery.

Page describes the next section over Bolt Tail to Bolt Head as 'the grandest in South Devon and also the most dangerous . . . Subsidences and pitfalls are many . . . the surface of the ground is uncertain . . . with crevasses on the very edge of the path.' It might almost be a glacier he is describing! The only road access to the cliff edge and the only footpath access to the sea's edge is half way at Sewer (Soar) Mill Sand. The clear weather view from Bolt Tail is said to extend to the Lizard. We set out eastward from the ancient earthwork here, looking forward eagerly to the delights of Page's Alpine-sounding dangers. Almost immediately comes Ramillies Cove, where a ship of the line was wrecked in 1760 with great loss of life. We climb up to Bolberry Down at over four hundred feet, where there is a smugglers' cave known as

H

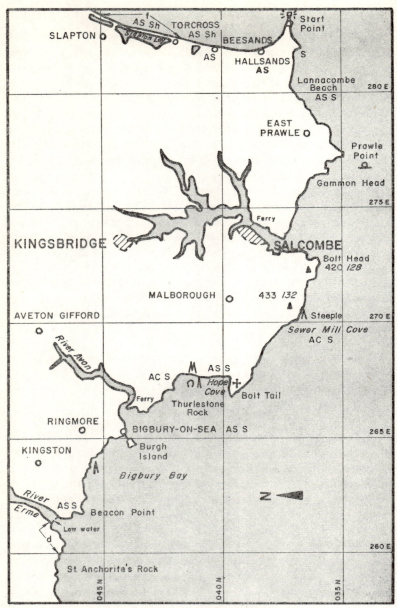

SLAPTON

TORCROSS
AS Sh
AS Sh
f
AS Sh
Slapton Ley

BEESANDS

Start
Point

AS

HALLSANDS
AS

S

Lannacombe
Beach
AS S

280 E

EAST
PRAWLE

Prawle
Point

Gammon Head

275 E

KINGSBRIDGE

Ferry

SALCOMBE

Bolt Head
420 128

MALBOROUGH

433 132

Steeple

270 E

AVETON GIFFORD

Sewer Mill Cove
AC S

River Avon

AC S

AS S

Hope
Cove

Bolt Tail

Ferry

Thurlestone
Rock

RINGMORE

BIGBURY-ON-SEA

AS S

265 E

KINGSTON

Burgh
Island

Bigbury Bay

N

River
Erme

AS S

Beacon Point

Low water

d

260 E

St Anchorite's Rock

045 N

040 N

035 N

St Anchorite's Rock to Slapton

(Based upon the Ordnance Survey Map, with the sanction of the Controller of HM Stationery Office, Crown Copyright reserved)

Ralph's Hole, and on to Vincents Pits—'great cracks and fissures between the path and the edge of the cliffs . . . many are fathomless'. A little further on, Rotten Pits are said to be similar. There have been frequent landslips at Slippery Point with nearby the trial shaft of a copper mine sunk in 1770. A mile ahead Sewer Mill Sand is reached over West Cliff and Cathole Cliff. This is a pleasant sandy beach with footpath access from the road above and some rocks around which almost make the grade for the climber. On the east side is a cavern said to communicate with Splat Cove at Salcombe. It is called Bull Hole for the animal which entered black and emerged white at the far end.

Offshore is the Ham Stone, but the truly amazing local rock is the Steeple, a foreshore pinnacle in Steeple Cove half a mile ahead. It is a grotesque twisted pillar, which would be a stiff climbing problem. The Path continues striding high at over four hundred feet to Bolt Head; here and there small rock masses give a muscle-exercising scramble to the passing traveller. The Path winds its way round the steep sides of Starehole Bay, where there is another lengthy cavern said to reach to Malborough Church, then picks its way among the fangy pinnacles of Sharpitor. Here, says Harper, 'the slatey stratification of the surrounding rocks lends itself to the most outlandish, hortent shapes of monstrous jibing faces, anvils, halberds, battle-axes and the likeness of a perfect armoury of magic weapons of offense'. We continue northwards along the Salcombe Estuary to join the road at Stink Cove, then pass through the urban area of Salcombe to find the ferry to East Portlemouth.

SALCOMBE (SX7338/39). Access by A381 from Kingsbridge Nearest stations—Totnes (19m) (scheduled bus service); Dartmouth (20½m). Ferry from East Portlemouth. Youth Hostel. E.C. Thurs.
'The Montpellier of England', says *Murray*'s *Guide*. First a fishing village, sending five ships to the siege of Calais; later a small shipbuilding centre. It has a fine sheltered harbour but an awkward bar at entry. Numerous boat trips are available on sea, estuary and up-river. Sandy beaches at North and South Sands, Mill Bay and Sunny Cove. *See*: Overbecks Museum and

Gardens (N.T.); Salcombe Castle (Henry VIII). *Visit*: Sharpitor and Bolt Head.

We cross by the ferry and set off southwards along the east bank of the estuary. Emerging once again on the seaward facing slopes, two miles of National Trust cliffs take us to Gammon Head, where two Spanish galleons went ashore and doubloons used to be found. The curious weathering of the local schists is seen to advantage hereabouts. Half a mile ahead is Prawle Point, the most southerly in Devon, referred to as 'Prol in Anglia' in a book written just after the Conquest. There is a Lloyd's Signal Station and an archway, 20ft high, which can be traversed in a boat on a calm day. Nearby is a tiny haven which fishing boats used to use. In the next section of three miles the Path runs along a raised beach, with a low wall to the present beach on one hand and crags and steep slopes of the former cliff line on the other. The village of East Prawle (road access) is on the cliff top. We pass Lannacombe Beach, which motorists reach by the roughest lane in Devon, and press on to the quieter sands of Matchcombe. There are some strange earth pinnacles here, formed where boulders on the raised beach have protected portions of it from subsequent erosion. This point can be reached by a footpath from the car park at the end of the Start Point road.

The Path now climbs and circles Peartree Point, beyond which loom the fantastic schistose ridges of Start Point, 'vertebrae of rocky pinnacles', says Page, 'seamed and fissured by the storms of ages, ribs of rock protruding through the grass descend to the cliffs in lines curiously regular'. We reach the lighthouse and find that this is an abrupt turning point in the coast.

A hundred years ago T. G. Bonney, the well known Alpine climber and geologist, wrote of Start: 'rarely, except in the recesses of the Alps, have I found a spot so perfect in its solitude or so impressive in its grandeur'. It is no longer so. Pinned to earth by the four hundred foot harpoons which radiate the local radio programmes, tramped on by Lilliputians from the car park, its jutting rocks tamed by lighthouse and radar, it sleeps quietly enough; however, since Bonney's time the Alps too have lost much of their solitude, so perhaps some parallel can still be drawn.

The Path runs north-west for a time, then north and soon we

reach Hallsands, to which there is road access. The original village near the sea's edge was all but destroyed during a great gale in 1917, because the beach level had been so reduced by the removal of shingle for use inland. Henceforward the cliffs are lower and there is a beach all the way. One mile on is Beesands with a triangular lake trapped behind a shingle bank, made, says Page, by the landlord of the Torcross Hotel for fishing. After skirting a quarry at the cliff edge the main road (A379) is joined at Torcross.

For two and a half miles to the north there stretches a shingle bank enclosing a freshwater lake known as Slapton Ley. The Path here must follow the road or the stones alongside it.

Bibliography

O.S. 1 inch Map Sheets 187 (Plymouth) and 188 (Torquay)
O.S. 2½ inch Map Sheets SX54, 64, 73, 83, 84
Fox, S. P., *Kingsbridge Estuary*, 1864
Luscombe, E., *Myrtles and Aloes* (Salcombe), 1861
Russell P. and York G., *Kingsbridge and Neighbourhood*, 1953
Nos. 4, 7, 8, 11, 26, 27, 37, 39, 44 from the General Bibliography

17

SLAPTON TO WATCOMBE HEAD
Slapton - Dartmouth - Kingswear - Berry Head - Brixham
Paignton - Torquay

THIS section includes a very considerable urban area of Paignton and Torquay, where no path will be designated. From Slapton to Berry Head is South Devon Area of Outstanding Natural Beauty; apart from 1½ miles of coast recently acquired near Dartmouth, there are no National Trust holdings, but the nature lover will no doubt be drawn to the Slapton Ley Field Centre and Bird Observatory, to the Zoo at Paignton and the aquarium at Torquay.

The shingle bar enclosing Slapton Ley consists of flints, quartz, and material from Dartmoor. It may be a miniature of Chesil Beach, but its origins appear to be obscure. From Blackpool to Sharkham Point Lower Devonian grits and shales form cliffs 'steep and often inaccessible'. 'The finest part of this coast', says Steers, 'with several stacks, lies between Stoke Fleming and the Dart, but that immediately eastwards of the Dart is more remote and less spoiled.' As usual the headlands arise from local strengthening of the rocks often by igneous materials—as at Matthew's Point, Redlap Cove, Combe Point, Compass Cove, and Inner and Outer Froward Points. Sharkham Point and Berry Head are limestone and there is limestone too on the far horn of Tor Bay at Hope's Nose, Daddy Hole, and so on. In between start the red Permian sandstones which are a typical feature of south-east Devon coast scenery. Babbacombe Bay shows a variety of rocks—dolerite, limestone, slates, etc, until the red sandstones and conglomerates start again north of Petit Tor Cove.

By the Path, Slapton to Dartmouth is 8 miles. One mile in urban Dartmouth leads to a ferry of 300yd to Kingswear. Kingswear to Brixham by the Path is 9½ miles and Brixham to Goodrington 3½ miles. Now there follows 6 miles through Paignton and Torquay for which public transport is available if required. The Path starts again opposite the Thatcher Stone, from which it is 4½ miles to Watcombe Head—a total Path length of 25½ miles.

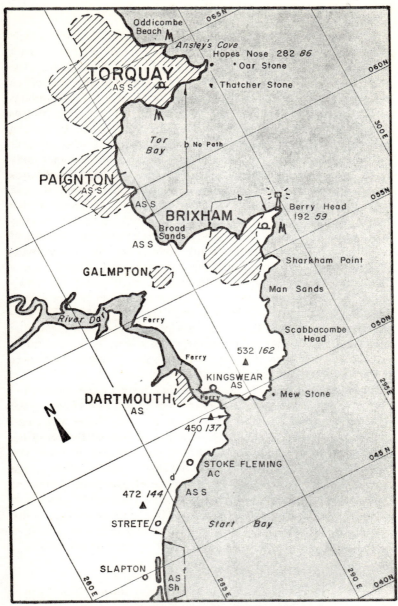

Slapton to Watcombe Head

(Based upon the Ordnance Survey Map, with the sanction of the Controller of **HM** Stationery Office, Crown Copyright reserved)

We set out northwards from Torcross by the road or the shingle alongside it. The freshwater Slapton Ley on our left is a quarter of a mile wide in places. In one and a half miles we reach a granite pillar erected by the US Army to acknowledge the use of an extensive area hereabouts for training for the Normandy landings in World War II. The five miles of beach stretching southwards from here for much of the way to Start Point could have been traversed on foot as an alternative route if required, while another two miles lead on to the point where the coastline becomes cliffy again below Strete. Where the hills begin the main road turns inland and climbs with a swinging flourish to the top; we can continue by a sloping trackway but this rejoins the road in due course. For the next two miles or so the Path faces the problem of avoiding contact as much as possible with this aggressive and sea-hugging road. In Strete (Youth Hostel) we take lesser roads inland leaving the main road nearer the sea. They coincide for a time, then at Landcombe the main road goes round Matthew's Point at the cliff edge while the Path takes a line further inland straight to Blackpool. There is a small shingle beach, with a sub-merged forest in the bay and a wooded valley inland. Again the main road takes a route close to the sea, while we go up the valley a short way and then cross by track to Stoke Fleming. The tower of the thirteenth-century church serves as a daymark.

Now the main road strikes almost due north to Dartmouth, the Path meanwhile following a trackway nearer the sea. However the actual cliff edge is not used until we get beyond Warren Point and our route is sometimes as much as half a mile from the coastline. At Blackstone Point we are on the edge of the Dart Estuary. Be-tween here and Dartmouth is Gallant's Bower, a 450ft hill with the ruins of a Civil War earthwork, the name of which recalls that of a similar feature near Clovelly. The summit commands a fine view of the town. The Path skirts the estuary-facing slopes to Dartmouth Castle, another of King Henry VIII's coastal defences, still in a good state of preservation. A mile along the riverside brings us to:

DARTMOUTH (SX8751). Access from the south-west by A379; a ferry brings A379 from the Torquay direction; there are ferries from the BR terminus at Kingswear. E.C. Weds.

There has been a port here since the Conquest; Rufus sailed for
Normandy in 1089, later two crusading expeditions left likewise.
The town sent thirty-one ships to the siege of Calais. A fierce
attack by the French was repelled in the reign of King Henry IV.
In Elizabethan times some of the adventurers lived and sailed
from here. Later it seems to have declined as Plymouth advanced.
Important American Forces Base in World War II. *See*: Quay
with ancient houses; the Butterwalk; Museum; Castle; Royal
Naval College; Bearscove Castle; Customs House; churches.
Visit: Dart Estuary and River by boat.

There is a choice of ferries to Kingswear on the east bank.

KINGSWEAR (SX8850/51). Access by A379 from Torquay. BR
main line terminus. Ferries to Dartmouth. E.C. Weds. *See*: Castle
(Henry VIII); Fort on Mount Ridley.

We follow the road along the estuary past Kingswear Castle to
Mill Bay Cove. The next section was voted by Harper 'the most
scrambly and tiring coastline in South Devon'. Burton comments
on the colours of the rocks: 'pink, grey, black, brown, red—there
is no end to the changing lights where rocks are polished by the
elements or deeply scarred'.

The *Red Guide* describes a route as far as Man Sands with the
added note, 'difficulties of right-of-way may make it necessary to
turn aside, but if these can be overcome by courteous enquiry and
regard for crops and gates, the walk is worth while'. The current
One Inch Map shows no trace of a path. It is intended that the
Path will hug the cliff edge by Downend Point and Scabbacombe
Sands to Crabrock Point, where there are some small caves in the
slates, and Man Sands. There is road and footpath access to this
point from Brixham. The Path continues along Southdown Cliff
to Sharkham Point and round St Mary's Bay to Durl Head, marked
by a long deserted iron mine; here there is a large cave, while
another running through the headland near the Mew Stone can be
traversed in a boat. Now we reach Berry head where the coast
turns sharply into Tor Bay.

The summit (191ft) is a fine viewpoint reaching out to Portland
Bill and over Tor Bay to the heights of Dartmoor. There is a

variety of rock climbing—some straighforward, some very hard indeed. There are remains of a Roman encampment, a cave, a squat lighthouse and the remains of a fort which used to protect Brixham. The outline of the Head is characteristically steep when seen from Tor Bay, to which it makes a most impressive portal. We descend to:

BRIXHAM (SX9255/56). Access by B3203 and B3205 off A379. Ferry from Torquay. Nearest station—Churston (2¼m). Youth Hostel at Galmpton (2m). E.C. Weds.
Important fishing port, the anchorage protected by a 3,000ft breakwater; now also a popular resort. William of Orange landed here on his way to the throne of England. In places, terraces of houses on steep slopes are linked by steps. *See*: Brixham (or Philp's) Cavern, 600ft long, where important archaeological finds were made; Museum. *Visit*: Berry Head; 8 beaches within 3 miles.

The Path continues close to the coastline crossing Churston Golf Course to Elbury Cove and Broad Sands. Soon the railway comes so close to the sea that the Path must needs give way to it. The designated route ends at Goodrington Village, beyond which are Goodrington Sands leading on to:

PAIGNTON (SX88/8960/61). Access by A379 from Kingswear, A379 from Torquay, A385 from Totnes. BR main line station. E.C. Weds.
A very popular modern resort with miles of fine sands and a pier. *See*: Zoo and Botanical Gardens; Parish Church; Museum.

There are houses all the way to:

TORQUAY (SXE90 to 93, N63 to 66). Access by A379 from Paignton, A379 from Teignmouth, A380 from Newton Abbot. BR main line station. Ferry from Brixham. E.C. Weds.
Now the major resort of the West Country. Torre Abbey was built in the years following the Conquest, but the fishing village nearby stayed small and unimportant for many centuries. A

writer in 1800 described the place as 'nothing more than a few cottages, with their little herb gardens, while beneath cluster the dwellings of fishermen, whose boats lie within the shelter of a rude pier, which gives the hamlet its name Tor Quay'. Then, during the Napoleonic Wars, Tor Bay was used as an anchorage by the fleet and thereafter it grew rapidly as a resort. There is rock climbing of a high standard on the cliffs here, while Kent's Cavern, also within the town boundaries, is a very important archaeological site which should on no account be missed, 'one of the oldest recognisable human dwellings in the country'. *See*: The Museum of the Torquay Natural History Society; Aquarium; Torre Abbey and Art Galley; Torre Abbey Meadows; Princess Gardens; Kent's Cavern; Rock Walk; harbour; numerous beaches and coves; Marine Spa; Cockington Court and Forge; Warberry Hill. *Visit*: Compton Castle (N.T. 4m W).

Though not designated as part of the Path the coast running east from Haldon Pier is well worthy of our attention. First comes a natural limestone arch called London Bridge. The top of the next headland is the plateau of Daddyhole Plain; the climbers' crags of Telegraph Hole Quarry, Daddy Hole, and Meadfoot Quarry are below. After this come Meadfoot Sands leading on to Kilmorie where the Path begins again. The line of islets offshore—Shag Rock, Thatcher Stone and Oar Stone mark the southern wall of a valley long ago attacked and submerged by the sea.

The Path runs over the headland of Hope's Nose to a fine and varied stretch of coastline running away northwards, a succession of coves and headlands in a range of rock types, which may be found considerably populated in the summer months. There are climbers' crags at Oddicombe and at Anstey's Cove, where one pinnacle has been likened to a feudal keep. The limestone ends at Petit Tor Point, beyond which the red cliffs continue for many miles. Below on the beach is a spiral sandstone rock—Lot's Wife.

Bibliography
O.S. 1 inch Map Sheet 188 (Torquay)
O.S. 2½ inch Map Sheets SX84, 85, 95, 86, 96
Town Guides from Dartmouth, Brixham, Paignton and Torquay
Russell, P., *Dartmouth*, 1950
Nos. 4, 7, 8, 11, 26, 27, 37, 39, 44 from the General Bibliography

18

WATCOMBE HEAD TO LADRAM BAY

Teignmouth - Dawlish - Exmouth - Budleigh Salterton
Ladram Bay

FROM Watcombe Head past the mouths of the Rivers Teign and Exe to a point some way beyond Exmouth, Permian rocks outcrop in 'fine, high and brightly coloured red cliffs'. The rock looks like dried mud and offers nothing to the climber except an occasional sea stack; even these are eroded comparatively rapidly. In the section between Teignmouth and Dawlish the railway at the cliff foot protects them from erosion, but the price is an almost complete loss of scenic attraction. There are unusual sand spits, should they interest you, at the mouths of both the Teign and the Exe. Red sandstone cliffs, now of the Trias, complete this coast section, forming a fine series of pinnacles at Ladram Bay. Noteworthy too, are the famous pebble beds in the cliff face on the other side of the mouth of the River Otter.

From just east of Exmouth, where the National Trust has a holding on Orcombe Cliff, onwards the coastline falls within the East Devon Area of Outstanding Natural Beauty. There is a National Wildfowl Refuge in the Exe Estuary.

This is one of the most broken sections of the Path—indeed, it hardly merits the title anywhere between Teignmouth and Exmouth. From Watcombe Head to Shaldon is 4 miles, whence a 330yd ferry takes us to Teignmouth. Now there is no designated route until the far side of Dawlish, and the gaps can if necessary be spanned by public transport. On foot it is two miles through urban Teignmouth and along the sea wall beside the railway to a point where the wall abuts an outjutting cliff and the rails enter a tunnel. There is no way round; the way over is blocked by houses, so we turn inland to the main road. Two miles of the road lead to the far side of urban Dawlish, where a mile of designated route cut off by the railway from the sea can be followed to Dawlish

138

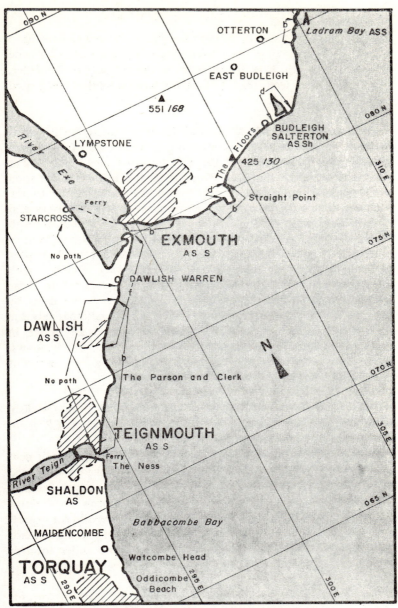

Watcombe Head to Ladram Bay

(Based upon the Ordnance Survey Map, with the sanction of the Controller of HM Stationery Office, Crown Copyright reserved)

Warren Station. The Path restarts beyond Exmouth and we have to bridge the gap by a ferry from Starcross, followed by a mile of urban Exmouth. Now it is 5 miles to the crossing of the Otter, and 3 miles more from there to Ladram Bay—a total of designated path miles of only 13.

Immediately alongside Watcombe Head is Watcombe Beach at the foot of the Valley of Rocks, impressive crags of sandstone conglomerate culminating in the well known Giant Rock. For a short way the Path lies back 200yd from the cliff edge. We soon reach Maidencombe and thenceforward the Path returns to the coastline. The road at a higher level is never very far away and at Labrador, a mile before Shaldon, they touch. Shaldon faces north across the Teign, nestling under the tree crowned red headland of the Ness. It is possible, says Harper, to traverse from Labrador to Shaldon round the foot of the Ness, 'the way is strewn with huge boulders of red conglomerate and is recommended to those who can best imitate the chamois in rock-leaping'. We cross by ferry to the tip of the Teignmouth shingle spit. Alternatively the former toll bridge, once said to be the longest road bridge in England (1,672ft), involves a detour of about a mile. The bye-laws, Payne tells us, prohibit driving an ass or rolling a cask across it and forbid bear-baiting, fives, football or tennis.

TEIGNMOUTH (SX93/9472/73). Access by A379 from Dawlish, A379 from Torquay and A381 from Newton Abbot. BR main line station. Ferry from Shaldon. E.C. Thurs.
Dating back at least to the twelfth century, Teignmouth sent seven ships to Edward III at Calais. It was sacked and burned by the French several times. Because of the extensive sands, sheltered site and equable climate began to grow as a resort in the early nineteenth century; still serves as a small port exporting china clay. *See*: The Den gardens; sea front which extends as a promenade alongside the railway for two miles towards Dawlish; sands and cliffs.

There is a certain uniformity of terrain as we proceed towards Dawlish on the sea wall. Eventually Hole Head blocks the way and the train takes to a tunnel; there is no walkers' route round

the Head and we have to move inland up Smugglers' Lane to join
A379 at Holcombe. Offshore are the remains of the Parson and
Clerk Rocks: 'the former', says Page, 'leans against the headland,
to which his shoulders are attached . . . Outside, completely surrounded by water, stands the Clerk, a tall pinnacle. He is more
venerable looking than his superior, for he is a favourite perch
for the gulls, and his head is quite white.' That was seventy years
ago. Slowly since and steadily the sea has been eroding them away.

Now about a mile of A379 seems unavoidable and there is no
pleasure whatsoever in walking beside a main road. Perhaps indeed
the best course is to take public transport from Teignmouth to
Dawlish, or even to Starcross, and leave this section of the coast
to the despoilers. The sea front at Dawlish extends past Lee Mount
to Coryton's Cove and it is possible at low water to carry on as
far as Shell Cove. Whether experienced coasteers could bridge the
gap at cliff foot between here and Smugglers' Lane is an unknown
quantity, but it is certain that there is no alternative for the walker
on the Path but to go round by the road.

DAWLISH (SX95/9676). Access by A379 from Exeter and A379
from Teignmouth. BR main line station. Information Bureau.
E.C. Thurs.
The guidebook says of it 'happy the town that has no history',
though it was in fact noted in the Domesday Book. The original
village was half a mile from the sea. Development as a resort
took place early in the nineteenth century around the valley
mouth. Extensive sands. See: Parson and Clerk Rocks; cliffs
and beaches.

The railway runs along the edge of the sands from end to end of
the town and then onwards towards the Exe. About a mile of
Path has been designated between the outskirts and Dawlish Warren
Station. The Warren is a sand bar partially blocking the mouth
of the River Exe. There are hutments and caravan parks, a holiday
camp and a 2,000-car park, so there is no incentive to linger. We
are faced with two miles on the road up the estuary to Starcross,
whence a ferry crosses the river to Exmouth. Looking back now
to the west, Esquiros tells us, 'one of the great features is the
Haldon Chain, which forms a background to the picture with its

mountainous peaks'. The alternative ferry from the tip of the Warren is not shown on the latest editions of maps.

EXMOUTH (SX9980, SY00/0180/81). Access by A377 from Exeter and A376 from Budleigh Salterton. BR branch line from Exeter. Ferry from Starcross. Information Bureau. E.C. Weds. Once a considerable port, having sent ten ships to Calais for Edward III; still a small commercial port at the present time. *The Guide to Watering Places* called it 'the oldest watering place in Devonshire . . . the heights of Haldon, on the west, which powerfully attract the damps too common in our climate, preserve Exmouth from that unpleasant humidity of atmosphere too prevalent in some parts of South Devon'. Now a modern resort with fine sands and amenities. *See*: Aquarium.

The esplanade extends for almost two miles along the Channel shore. The designated Path skirts the cliff edge round High Land of Orcombe. Sandy Bay to the east is backed by an extensive caravan site. The Path cuts across the base of Straight Point and beyond Littleham Cove climbs to the top of a high cliff, more than four hundred feet, called The Floors. There are fine views along the coast and a high-reaching golf course. A pleasant path over open cliff tops leads gently down into:

BUDLEIGH SALTERTON (SY05/0681/82). Access by A376 from Exmouth and from Newton Poppleford on A38. Nearest station —Exmouth (4½m). E.C. Thurs. There was a village in the thirteenth century, but the resort is entirely modern. Two miles of beach composed of large pebbles. *Visit*: Birthplace of Sir W. Raleigh at Hayes' Barton (3m); Bicton Gardens at East Budleigh (2m).

Immediately beyond the town the route along the sea's edge is barred by the River Otter. Paths do indeed approach the mouth from either hand and it is certainly narrow, but as a boat may seldom be available it is usually necessary to detour inland to the first bridge three-quarters of a mile upstream. This river was formerly much larger, for Leland noted in his travels, 'Less than an hunderith yeres sins shippes usid this haven, but it is now clean

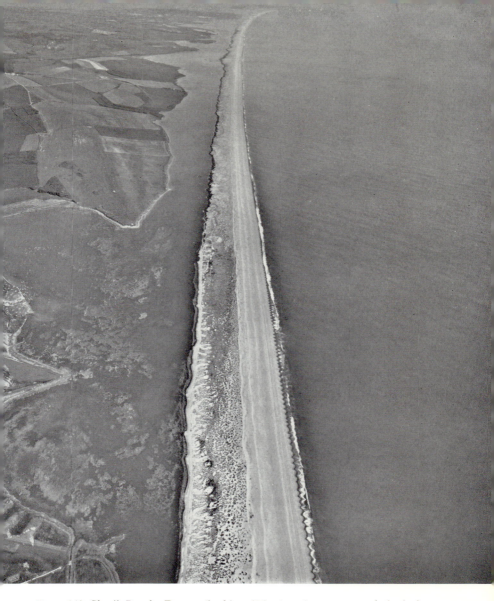

Page 143 Chesil Beach, Dorset (looking SE). A unique geomorphological feature, this huge bank of shingle divides the sea on the right from the waters of the Fleet on the left. It terminates in the far distance at the Isle of Portland

Page 144 The Foreland, Dorset (looking SW). The Old Harry Rocks are in the foreground with other chalk pinnacles further on below the cliffs leading to Swanage Bay. The chalk ridge of Ballard Down, which terminates the Purbeck Hills, forms the near portal of the Bay.

barred'. In the cliff face nearby are the famous pebble beds of Budleigh Salterton, mostly quartzite and grit, the stones from which have been carried by the eastward longshore drift to beaches all the way along the Channel coast, even as far as Dungeness.

The Path continues along the cliff edge to Ladram Bay, where there is a sandy beach with caves and a unique collection of sandstone pinnacles—six in and around the bay, a seventh further off below High Peak. In Page's time one of the big pinnacles was an arch, but in 1925 the irresistible forces of sea erosion reduced it to the present form. There are extensive caravan parks here and exploration of the natural amenities is perhaps best left until the off-season. There is road access and a large car park.

Bibliography

O.S. 1 inch Map Sheets 188 (Torquay) and 176 (Exeter)
O.S. 2½ inch Map Sheets SX96, 97, SY08
Town Guides from Teignmouth, Dawlish, Exmouth and Budleigh Salterton
Delderfield, E. R., *Exmouth Milestones*, 1948
Nos. 4, 7, 8, 11, 26, 27, 37, 39, 45 from the General Bibliography

I

19

LADRAM BAY TO LYME REGIS
Sidmouth - Branscombe - Beer - Seaton

THERE are no sharp indentations in this section of Lyme Bay; the cliffs, sometimes spectacular and of variegated colourings, are in new softer rocks, which are subject to erosion and offer nothing to the rock climber. Beach traverses are possible in many places for the walker tired of the cliff top, but as he goes he must keep a sharp eye on the state of the slopes above him. The resorts of Sidmouth, Seaton, and Lyme Regis cater between them for a wide variety of tastes.

The rocks are Trias at first, but as we move eastwards we find more and more Cretaceous beds. Chalk appears on the upper slopes at Upper Dunscombe Cliff by Salcombe Regis and forms its first headland at Beer Head. There is a more or less continuous shingle beach, mostly chert and flint, below the cliffs from Peak Hill by Ladram Bay through to Branscombe Mouth. Some sand appears at low water. Eastwards from Branscombe is the famous landslip area of East Devon, the notable sites being at Hooken Cliff by Beer Head (1790), at Dowlands, east of Seaton (1839) and at Whitlands, still further east (1765). The falls have taken place where Cretaceous rocks rest uncomfortably on Lias or Trias, and where the junction is close to sea level and sloping slightly seawards. Erosion by the sea removes the support for the upper beds which slide over the lower. At Dowlands, for example, eight million tons of rock subsided at one time, leaving a new inland cliff 200ft high and raising offshore a ridge of Upper Greensand 40ft high and three-quarters of a mile long.

The whole of this stretch of coastline, except for the urban areas of the three principal resorts is included in the East Devon Area of Outstanding Natural Beauty. The National Trust owns some small properties at Sidmouth and a substantial cliff section between Salcombe Regis and Branscombe Mouth, as well as a mile of foreshore at the latter. The Undercliff between Axmouth and Lyme Regis is a National Nature Reserve.

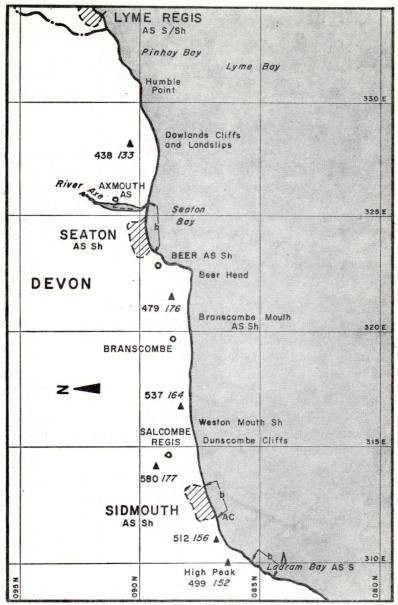

LYME REGIS
AS S/Sh

Pinhay Bay

Lyme Bay

Humble
Point

330 E

Dowlands Cliffs
and Landslips

▲
438 *133*

River Axe   AXMOUTH
AS

325 E

Seaton
Bay

b

SEATON
AS Sh

DEVON

BEER AS Sh

Beer Head

▲
479 *176*

Branscombe Mouth
AS Sh

320 E

○
BRANSCOMBE

N ◀

537 *164*
▲

Weston Mouth Sh

SALCOMBE
REGIS

Dunscombe Cliffs

315 E

▲ ○
580 *177*

SIDMOUTH
AS Sh

b

AC

512 *156* ▲

310 E

b

Ladram Bay AS S

▲
High Peak
499 *152*

095 N   090 N   085 N   080 N

Ladram Bay to Lyme Regis

(Based upon the Ordnance Survey Map, with the sanction of the Controller of HM Stationery Office, Crown Copyright reserved)

By the Path it is 2½ miles from Ladram Bay to Sidmouth. The urban area of Sidmouth occupying half a mile is separated from the one mile urban area of Seaton by an 8-mile stretch of Path. From Seaton to Lyme Regis by the Path is 6 miles, while the urban area of the latter occupies a further mile—a total distance of 16½ miles of Path.

From the six pinnacles and the caravans of Ladram Bay we climb steadily up the lofty High Peak (499ft), which is surmounted by a camp. Offshore is the seventh pinnacle, Big Picket Rock, accessible by the foreshore at low water. Harper recommended a boat trip along this section, 'rowed by one of the Sidmouth boatmen who have pachydermatous hands'. Nowadays they probably have motors. The view from the headland extends from Portland Bill to Sharkham Point by Dartmouth. 'Anywhere else', says Page, 'the beautiful colouring of red rock and clear green water would excite remark; but in this land of gorgeous hues the eye becomes sated, and one only exclaims at some tit-bit of special loveliness. Such a tit-bit is High Peak, the most beautiful cliff in South Devon.' The Path passes along to Peak Hill (512ft) then makes a straightforward descent to Sidmouth, 'situated betwen two romantic Alpine hills at the mouth of the little River Sid'.

SIDMOUTH (SY1287/88/89). Access from A35 by B3175 or B3176. Nearest station—Honiton (10m). E.C. Thurs.
Sent three ships to Edward III at Calais. Later described by Leland as 'a fisshear town, with a broke of that name, and a bay'; the harbour was eventually choked by sand. Began to rise as a resort in the early nineteenth century; an 1820 guidebook says of it 'with respect to accommodation Sidmouth has to boast of a good ballroom; and on the beach is a billiard table'. Now it is one of the most charming resorts of the whole Channel coast. The beach is shingle, described ninety years ago by *Black*'s *Guide* as 'rich in valuable stones, such as chalcedony, agates, and jaspers, of different kind and colour'. There is some sand at low water.

We climb from the Alma Bridge over the River Sid up the easterly 'alpine hill', Salcombe Hill, which reaches to over 500ft. In a mile a descent is made into the valley below Salcombe Regis. This is followed by the 500ft Dunscombe Cliff, where high up we find the most westerly coastal chalk. Hereabouts Ramshorn Rocks outcrop in an impressive crag on the cliff face. These are not obviously suitable for the climber, but is this perhaps the same chalk which Frenchmen climb in the valley of the Seine above Rouen? Down we go again into a second deep valley, Weston Combe, which has a caravan park well hidden on its upper slopes. Somewhere here there are petrifying streams on the cliffs, but so difficult of access that, says Harper, 'weaker brethren purchase such specimens of moss, bramble, and so on, as they may at Branscombe, and on their return home, yarn about the Alpine difficulties of discovering them'. All this section so far could be traversed on the beach even at high tide and we could continue with equal facility to Branscombe Mouth, except that the seaward slopes here are dotted with shacks.

The Path climbs over the next top (537ft) and in two miles we reach Branscombe; passing between the village and the cliff edge through the camp of Branscombe Castle, we reach sea level again at Branscombe Mouth (road access). This is a narrow opening between high cliffs; the valley trifurcates immediately inland, the most southerly arm running almost parallel to the cliff edge back to Branscombe Village. There is an ancient church.

The cliffs beyond reach once again to over 400ft at South Down Common and in a mile comes the outjutting Beer Head, a 400ft bastion of chalk with a view over a hundred miles of coastline from Start Point to Portland Bill. The colouring is wonderful in the range of contrasting tints; as Page tells us: 'You have the yellow cliffs of Dorset; the ochres and siennas of those about Axmouth; the white and grey of Beer; the red of Sidmouth and Dawlish; while the limestone of Berry Head has become a pale blue, and the grim rocks of Start a line of softest grey.' Below South Down Common is the landslip area of Hooken Cliff, where in the great fall of 1790 several acres of ground dropped more than 200ft vertically, breaking up into columns and pinnacles and moving 200yd towards the sea. The Path from Branscombe takes a series of narrow ways through the lush vegetation of this undercliff. Close to the Head an extremely steep path runs almost straight down to Little Beach at about the highest angle at which walking is possible. It seems likely that a route could be made from Branscombe to Beer at the cliff foot, but it would be for coasteers rather than walkers. From Beer Head straightforward paths lead down to Beer passing en route a large caravan park, which seems reasonably unobtrusive coming from this direction even though it almost fills the view from Seaton way.

BEER (SY2289). Access by B3172 and B3174 from A35. Nearest station—Axminster (8m). Youth Hostel. E.C. Thurs.
There was a port and a pier at one time; the pier had just been destroyed when Leland came by in the 1580s. Later a notorious smuggling centre. *Visit*: the quarries on the Branscombe road— a quarter of a mile underground at a depth of 300ft—from which the stone was obtained for Exeter Cathedral among others (guide advised); sea caves reached by boat are said to communicate with the quarries.

Round the next chalk headland, White Cliff, we come quickly to:

SEATON (SY23/2489/90). Access by B3172 from A35. Nearest station—Axminster (7m). E.C. Thurs.
Mentioned in the Domesday Book and sending two ships to the siege of Calais in 1347, by Leland's time the harbour was blocked by a shingle bank much as it is today. 'Ther hath been a very notable haven at Seaton, but now ther lyith between the two points of the old haven a mighty rigge and barre of pible stones in the very mouth of it, and the River Axe is driven to the very est point of the haven caullid Whitclif, and ther at a very small gut goith into the sea.' Nowadays a pleasant modern resort with caravan parks, holiday camps, etc.

The Path begins again at the east end of the town at the bridge over the Axe. Axmouth is now over half a mile inland. It seems certain that this was once an important seaport for hereabouts starts the Great Ridgeway—a prehistoric trackway which has been traced through Dorset, over Salisbury Plain, along the Berkshire Downs and the Chilterns and through East Anglia to the Wash. The change seems to have been brought about by a large cliff fall in the twelfth or thirteenth centuries. During the 1800s, a canal was planned from Bristol through to Axmouth, which would save ships from having to make the dangerous passage round Land's End. A copper bolt in the wall of the church marks one of the survey stations, but there was never a canal.

From the Axe bridge the Path climbs away up the next hill, diverging at first from the cliff edge, then returning half a mile ahead by a footpath. Soon we drop over the edge into the largest of the landslip areas, which is continuous almost as far as Lyme Regis. The great slip of 1839, which, wrote Dr Buckland, 'far exceeds the ravages of the earthquakes of Calabria and almost the vast volcanic fissures of the Vol de Bove on the flanks of Etna', involved about a mile of Bindon and Dowland Cliffs by Culverhole Point. Twenty acres of the cliff top subsided seawards leaving a new rock face 200ft high above a chasm varying from 200 to 400ft wide. Some cottages went with the rest, the inhabitants escaping just in time, some cultivated fields also, from which the crops were duly garnered in the following autumn. Steep walls, pinnacles and huge chalk blocks make for striking scenery. 'From below', says the *Thorough Guide*, 'it is easy to fancy oneself gazing at some huge ivy mantled castle. We seem to occupy the outside of the deep moat, neglected and well-nigh filled by a tangled growth of underwood and creepers. Across it rises a many-bastioned wall, festooned and almost hidden in ivy. Along the top of that we see the main platform, whence tower, stern and abrupt, the walls of the fortress.' Now there is a considerable Nature Reserve here, giving a unique opportunity for the study of the development of self-sown vegetation.

The Path continues in the undercliff past Rousdon to Whitlands Cliffs, where slips took place in 1765 and again in 1840, and where, says Harper, 'the explorer requires not a little of the suppleness and agility of the chamois, and growing at last weary of bounding hazardously from crag to crag, climbs with extraordinary labour, past monstrous grey, ivy-grown spires and pinnacles of limestone'. Small changes are always possible and the line is likely to change from year to year as the terrain moves. At Pinhay the undercliff shows three ridges and gullies parallel to the coast, between the main cliff and the sea. 'Pinhay', wrote Jane Austen, 'with its green chasms between romantic rocks, where a scene so wonderful and so lovely is exhibited, as may more than equal any of the resembling scenes of the far-famed Isle of Wight.' The sandstone pinnacle of Chimney Rock below Ware is only a few yards short of the Devon-Dorset border. We cross over into the latter and descend by footpaths to the Cobb at Lyme Regis.

Bibliography

O.S. 1 inch Map Sheets 176 (Exeter) and 177 (Taunton and Lyme Regis)
O.S. 2½ inch Map Sheets SY08, 18, 28(29), 39
Town Guides from Sidmouth and Seaton
Butters, F. C., *Branscombe, the parish and church*, 1949
Griffiths I., *Inside England: on the Borders of Dorset and Devon*, 1968
Nos. 4, 7, 8, 11, 26, 27, 37, 39, 45 from the General Bibliography

20

LYME REGIS TO ABBOTSBURY
Lyme Regis - Charmouth - Golden Cap - West Bay
Bridport - Burton Bradstock - Abbotsbury

BLACK VEN between Lyme Regis and Charmouth is another notable landslip area. From Lyme the coastline is concave for a mile and a half to Charmouth and thereafter runs in a near straight line for some fourteen miles to Abbotsbury. The rocks are limestones and blue and yellow shales of the Lias, which outcrop almost horizontally, capped in places by greensands and chalk of the Cretaceous. In the neighbourhood of Bridport are bright yellow Bridport Sands. This coast is a 'geological paradise', says the *Thorough Guide*, 'and fossils abound from shells to saurian monsters'. The famous Chesil Beach begins at Bridport and runs for 18 miles to the bulky block of the Isle of Portland. In this section it is continuously attached to the cliffs, but further on a freshwater lake known as the Fleet separates it from the main mass of the land. At this end the pebbles are fine sand grains; they increase steadily in size throughout the length until at Portland they are as large as potatoes. The local man is said to know his whereabouts on the Beach from the dimensions of the stones underfoot.

All this is Dorset Area of Outstanding Natural Beauty. The National Trust owns a particularly extensive coastline area stretching from Charmouth to Eype Mouth, as well as smaller areas at Burton Bradstock and by West Bexington.

By the Path Lyme Regis to Seatown is 5 miles, Seatown to Burton Bradstock is 5½ miles and Burton Bradstock to West Bexington 3½ miles. Henceforward there are three alternatives, two of them designated as routes for the Path. The traveller who hugs the coast to Abbotsbury is later faced with the urban area of Weymouth. He who turns inland at West Bexington will follow inland ridges looking down on the sea, which is not regained until the far side of Weymouth Bay. Whichever the route, about 3½ miles of it are included herewith, making a total path length of 17½ miles.

153

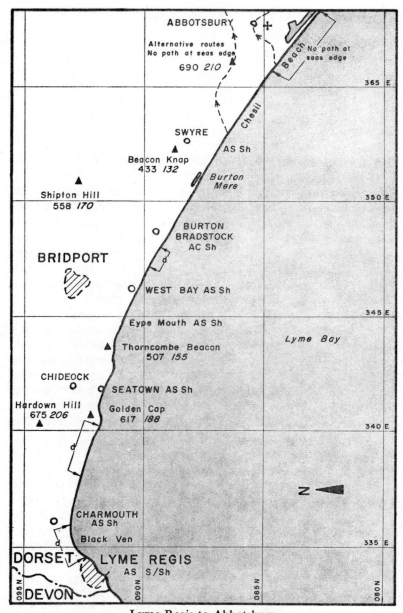

ABBOTSBURY

Alternative routes
No path at seas edge
690 *210*

No path at
seas edge

365 E

Chesil Beach

SWYRE

AS Sh

Beacon Knap
433 *132*

Burton
Mere

350 E

Shipton Hill
558 *170*

BURTON
BRADSTOCK
AC Sh

BRIDPORT

d

WEST BAY AS Sh

345 E

Eype Mouth AS Sh

Lyme Bay

Thorncombe Beacon
507 *155*

CHIDEOCK

SEATOWN AS Sh

Hardown Hill
675 *206*

Golden Cap
617 *188*

340 E

d

N

CHARMOUTH
AS Sh

Black Ven

335 E

DORSET LYME REGIS
AS S/Sh

DEVON

095 N

060 N

085 N

080 N

Lyme Regis to Abbotsbury

(*Based upon the Ordnance Survey Map, with the sanction of the Controller of HM
Stationery Office, Crown Copyright reserved*)

LYME REGIS (SY33/3491/92). Access by A35 from Bridport, by A35 from the west and A3070 from the north. Nearest station— Axminster (6m). E.C. Thurs.

Mentioned first in Saxon records. The stone pier, known as the Cobb, forming the harbour was erected in the reign of Edward I. Lyme Regis sent four ships to the siege of Calais. Later the Cobb was destroyed by heavy seas and rebuilt by a levy. The town sent ships against the Armada and troops were sent to defend it from invasion. Scene of a protracted siege in the Civil War; later Monmouth landed on the Cobb on his way to Sedgemoor and Tower Hill. Lyme has always been an important site for fossils, found on the cliffs on either hand. There is a shingle beach with some sand at low water. 'The houses,' Treves tells us, 'like the Gadarene swine, appear to be running down a steep place into the sea. At the end of the street they are only prevented from tumbling into the ocean by a sudden sea-wall, over which they hang unsteadily.' *See*: Aquarium; Museum; Parish Church.

The route runs by path and minor road over Black Ven, where landslipping carried the coast road into the sea in 1924. Perhaps 'Ye Plimlimon of Dorsetshire' which the local historian noted here-abouts in the eighteenth century, has also disappeared the same way. Now there is the usual undercliff, but the Path stays above the inland cliff line. In 1908 'Lyme Volcano' erupted on this under-cliff, iron pyrites and bituminous shales igniting spontaneously by the action of water and emitting sulphurous smoke over a period of some months. Camden noted a similar phenomenon here in 1751 'after very hot weather'. From Black Ven the Path descends to Charmouth, which lies, says Norway, 'in a broad low cleft at the foot of great hills. Beyond one sees a succession of dark and jagged cliffs which need only a grey sky and the shadow of a thin mist clinging round their summits to give them the mystery and grandeur of a mountain line.'

CHARMOUTH (SY3693). Access by A35 from Lyme Regis and by A35 from Bridport. Nearest station—Axminster (5½m). E.C. Thurs.

Mentioned in Saxon records and in the Domesday Book. Now a

pleasant small resort with shingle and sand at low water. Another notable fossil site. *Visit*: Black Ven; Golden Cap.

The Path climbs away from Charmouth along the cliff edge and in three-quarters of a mile we enter on a fine continuous stretch of National Trust property, which is named for Golden Cap, the high outstanding yellow-capped hill a mile or two ahead. The property starts at another small landslipped area known as Cain's Folly, above which the Path hugs the cliff edge. After crossing some small streams we come over Broom Cliff to St Gabriel's Mouth, where the shingle beach can be reached by a steep path. The beach is continuous at low water and it could be traversed to Lyme Regis on the one hand or West Bay on the other by anyone prepared to tackle that sort of going. One would get a fine view of the cliffs and stand a good chance of finding fossils; the rocks are however rotten and would need watching.

The Path tackles no such risky ventures but climbs instead past the ruins of Stratton St Gabriel Church to the magnificent viewpoint of Golden Cap, which rises hard by to 617ft. The grey and blue Lias here is capped by the golden Upper Greensand, which gives a startling colour contrast and the name. Below is an extensive under-cliff called Wear (or Shorn) Cliff. Easy tracks lead down on the far side to a few cottages and an inn at Seatown (road access), which is an outlier of Chideock on the A35 three-quarters of a mile inland. On the far side of the gap the cliffs begin to climb once again and, passing the length of Doghouse Hill, we reach Thorncombe Beacon (507ft) at the cliff edge, which is also capped with Upper Greensand, though presumably less obviously so. From it the Path descends to Eype Mouth (road access).

West Bay, the seaside and port of Bridport, is a mile away over the golden West Cliff, which is yellow Lias sandstone capped with Oolitic limestone.

WEST BAY (SY45/4690). Access from Bridport by minor road. Nearest station—Bridport (1½m). E.C. Thurs.
Formerly called Bridport Harbour. The harbour is at the mouth of the River Brit, the banks of which are prolonged by jetties. The present arrangements date from the early nineteenth century; it was never previously being of any importance. Now a small resort

with a shingle beach, and centre for fossils. Extensive caravan site.

One and a half miles up river is:

BRIDPORT (SY46/4792/93). On A35. BR branch line from West-
bury. Youth Hostel. E.C. Thurs.
The history goes back to Saxon times, when there was a mint and
a priory hereabouts, and has continued to be varied though not
outstanding. It has for a long time been an important centre for
rope-making. *See*: Museum; Art Gallery.

The gap in the cliffs at West Bay is only six hundred yards wide
and the Path is soon climbing away again over another giant
fossiliferous yellow cliff, known as East Cliff, which has a golf
course at the top. In about a mile we reach the mouth of the River
Bride, with shingle beach and caravan camp; Burton Bradstock
is a short way upstream. A detour is involved before the stream
can be crossed.

BURTON BRADSTOCK (SY4889). On B3157 from Bridport to Weymouth. Nearest station—Bridport (3m). E.C. Thurs.
A mermaid came ashore here in 1757, says Hutchins. *See*:
Church. *Visit*: Shipton Hill (2m NE), which has a remarkable
resemblance to an enormous ship lying on the summit keel
uppermost.

Burton Cliff, another bright yellow one, rises between the village
and the sea. After Cliff End the slope of the cliffs becomes easy;
the road climbs up to higher ground and to Swyre, but the Path
continues at the foot of the slope just above the beach. We are now
alongside the early part of the great Chesil Beach which curves
gently away towards the distant Isle of Portland. Burton Mere
is a foretaste of the great lakes behind the Beach which we shall
reach further on; here as later the Path runs behind the water.
Below West Bexington, some three miles from Burton, there is
road access to the sea's edge and this is the parting of the ways
between the inland ridge route and the coastline route, which only
join again beyond Weymouth. There is a Youth Hostel three miles
inland at Litton Cheney.

The former route has troubles in avoiding roads, but is reasonably successful in doing so. From West Bexington Limekiln Hill is traversed mostly by path; we cross the road (B3157) at Tulk's Hill and by way of Abbotsbury Castle earthwork reach tracks over Wears Hill and White Hill. Here, with a view down into Abbotsbury in the valley beneath, we leave the continuation of the route for our next section.

The coastwise alternative continues immediately above the Beach to a point close to Abbotsbury. Now we follow a track inland, contouring Chapel Hill surmounted by St Catherine's Chapel—a shipping landmark, to Abbotsbury Village.

ABBOTSBURY (SY5785). On B3157 between Bridport and Weymouth. Nearest station—Weymouth (9m). E.C. Thurs.
The monastery here was founded in the eleventh century, suppressed by Henry VIII and garrisoned and sacked during the Civil War. Only fragments remain. *See*: Church; Abbey Barn (reed-thatched) and monastic ruins; the Swannery—the largest in Europe, dating back to Saxon times; sub-tropical Gardens; St Catherine's Chapel.

Bibliography

O.S. 1 inch Map Sheets 177 (Taunton and Lyme Regis), 178 (Dorchester)
O.S. 2½ inch Map Sheets SY39, 49(48), 58
Folder Map/Guide Golden Cap (National Trust)
Town Guides from Lyme Regis and Bridport
Maskell, J., *The History and Topography of Bridport*, Bridport, 1855
Wanklyn, C., *Lyme Regis: a retrospect*, Hatchards, 1927
Nos. 23, 27, 38, 39, 40, 51 from the General Bibliography

21

ABBOTSBURY TO DURDLE DOOR

Hardy Monument - Maiden Castle - Weymouth Horse
The Fleet - Chesil Beach - Portland Bill - Weymouth
Ringstead Bay - White Nothe - Durdle Door

AT Abbotsbury the Chesil Beach first becomes separated from the coastline. Henceforward the Fleet, varying in width between 200 and 1,000yd, stretches on behind the Beach until it reaches the sea at Small Mouth through the causeway connecting the Isle of Portland with the mainland. The Beach is 200yd wide and 43ft high at Portland; 170yd wide and 23ft high at Abbotsbury. The shingle reaches 6 fathoms below low water at Abbotsbury and 8 at Portland. We have already remarked on the end to end grading of the component pebbles, which are mainly flints, mixed with limestones from Portland and Purbeck and stones from Devon and Cornwall. 'No part of the English coast', says Treves, 'has seen more numerous or more fatal wrecks than has Chesil Beach . . . when the sea gives up her dead it will be a host unaccountable who will crowd the steep sides of the amphitheatre of Deadman's Bay.' This was also a notorious site for wreckers.

The Isle of Portland is a massive outcropping of Jurassic limestone. Beyond Weymouth the coastline is mainly Jurassic clays and grits until White Nothe where the chalk comes in again. For the rest of this section the main cliffs are of chalk, while the limestone which outcrops in a parallel line to the south forms first a series of reefs, then in the middle of St Oswald's Bay the impressive arch of Durdle Door.

Of the alternative route for the Path in this section, the inland way lies entirely within the Dorset Area of Outstanding Natural Beauty; the traveller on the coastwise way leaves it for several miles in and around Weymouth. There are important Nature sites at Abbotsbury—the Swannery—at Radipole Lake near Weymouth and, just off the Path, on the Isle of Portland. The National Trust owns the Hardy Monument, passed on the inland route,

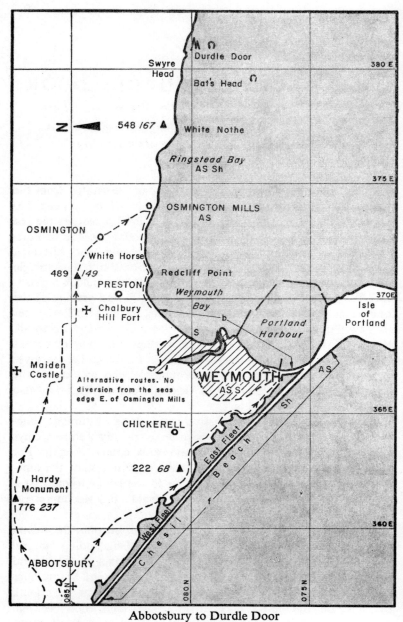

Abbotsbury to Durdle Door

and nearly half a mile of cliff between Ringstead Bay and White Nothe.

From White Hill above Abbotsbury it is 7½ miles to Ridgeway Hill on the Dorchester to Weymouth road and a further 6½ miles to Osmington Mills where this route rejoins the coastline. By the Path along the inner edge of the Fleet it is 6½ miles to Fleet Village and a further 4½ miles to Sandsfoot Castle above Portland Harbour where the designated route ends. The traveller following the Beach itself would continue straight ahead where the route of the previous section turned inland to Abbotsbury, thus saving a mile or so; thenceforward his route is a bee line and shorter than the windings of the inner edge of the Fleet. It will certainly be harder going however. A circuit of the Isle of Portland, not actually part of the Path, would involve another 11 miles. Beyond Weymouth the designated route begins again at Overcombe, when it is 3 miles to Osmington Mills. Now all routes coincide and 5 miles of cliff edge bring us to Durdle Door. The total Path distance by either route is about 19 miles.

The inland route offers for the only time on the Path a way over chalk hills with the typical vegetation, the short grass, the spacious views and the antiquities. It successfully overcomes the problems of the roads, avoiding them to a very substantial extent. Along the ridge of White Hill we come to a steep road climbing out of Abbotsbury; immediately north is the stone circle 'Grey Mare and her Colts', there are other monoliths and barrows around. On the far side of the road trackways lead on to Portesham Hill on the Portesham to Winterbourne Abbas road. This too is crossed to Ridge Hill where there is a dolmen, the Hell Stone, nine upright stones re-erected in the last century. Half a mile away on Black Downs is the 74ft Hardy Monument, a magnificent viewpoint. This 'grey wide-mouthed factory chimney', says the Shell *Guide*, 'is an admirable sea mark'. Treves, too, saw it as a factory chimney or 'a strange resemblance to a telephone receiver placed on end'. It commemorates Thomas Masterman Hardy, naval colleague of Horatio Nelson, and not, as one might perhaps expect, Dorset's own poet and novelist. There is road access to this point also, but the Path swings south-east and then east over Bronkham Hill and Great Hill to cross B3159 at Gould's Bottom; there

K

are tumuli, earthworks and other antiquities to enliven the way.

At this point Maiden Castle, the greatest British earthwork, is only a mile or so to the north. It is well worth the detour. The pattern is oval, 400yd by 900yd; there are never less than three separate defence lines and the entrances are ingeniously staggered. The central area has remained undisturbed since Roman times, escaping the plough even in the great wars of the twentieth century.

After the crossing of B3159 another half mile brings us to A354; the road opposite is avoided by a 300yd detour to the south where we finally cross both main road and railway and press on eastwards over Bincombe Down. After a short spell on a minor road the Path turns off right again and crosses to Bincombe Village below Bincombe Hill, which carries several tumuli. It continues on tracks passing close to the Iron Age Charlbury Camp, a single bank and ditch with pit dwellings. We touch on the road once again by Green Hill, then strike up White Horse Hill which has a steep south-facing scarp above Sutton Poyntz. Here is one of the best known of the hill figures, cut in the chalk in 1808. A horseman, 280ft long and 323ft high, it is said to represent George III, who first popularised Weymouth. He is depicted riding away from it! The Path descends to Osmington Village, crosses A353, and regains the coast by a path to Osmington Mills.

On the coastal alternative, the Path from Abbotsbury does not at first touch the edge of the Fleet, but continues along the hills above passing north of Clayhanger and north of Wyke Wood, before making for the water by way of Bridge Lane. From here to Small Mouth the route follows the edge of the Fleet, the Beach across the way cuts off the view of the sea. There is road access by Langton Herring and again by East Fleet. Eventually we come, depressingly, into the environs of Weymouth.

The alternative by the Beach needs no description. It is long, hard going and monotonous, but it is an 'expedition', for once embarked upon the route must be completed or retraced. It is not a place for bad weather, for the waves have been known to sweep over the top, carrying with them on at least one occasion a small boat. Along the eight miles the map shows three ferries which might, if working, be used for escape.

In the early years of the last century before the bridge and causeway were built across Small Mouth to Portland the nearest way from Weymouth was 'to be ferried over an inlet of the sea at the end of Smallmouth Sands. Portland is worth a visit by the passing traveller, the circuit being about eleven miles. It is entirely limestone, a fine building material which has been extensively quarried, and is notably bare; in places the rock consists entirely of compacted sea shells. There is rock climbing and a cave or two. The Bill of Portland (lighthouse, seamark, Pulpit Rock, etc) at the south end is a notable place of pilgrimage, offshore is the famous Portland Race marked for mariners by the Shambles Lightship, which is to be replaced in the near future by a huge modern navigational buoy.

From Small Mouth the Path is designated as far as the fragmentary ruins of Sandsfoot Castle. There is no route through Weymouth.

WEYMOUTH (E66 to 68, N76 to 80). Access by A353 (east), A354 (north) and B3157 (west). BR main line station. Information Bureau. E.C. Weds.

The history goes back to the fourteenth century. Formerly Weymouth and Melcombe Regis were separate towns on either side of the River Wey. In Leland's time there was no bridge but a boat attached to a swinging rope, 'in the ferry boote they used no ores'. The importance of Weymouth as a watering place dates from the reign of George III. 'Immersion in the briny flood is safe and delightful,' says the early guidebook. 'The sands are as smooth as a carpet, and solid to the tread, while the bathing machines, upwards of forty in number, are in constant requisition from six in the morning till noon. They are drawn into the sea by a horse to the necessary depth, and are attended by proper guides.' Now it is a substantial resort with sandy beaches facing east and south-east. There is a modern port with steamer services to the Channel Isles. To the south between here and Portland is the naval anchorage of Portland Harbour. *See*: Piers and Harbour; Radipole Lake; Sandsfoot Castle. *Visit*: Isle of Portland; Chesil Beach; the White Horse; Chalbury.

The Path escapes from the main road at Overcombe by a track

over Furzy Cliff which passes the site of a Roman temple on Jordon Hill. Inland at Preston are found a Roman tessellated pavement and an ancient pack-horse bridge. At Bowleaze Cove we come to some caravan camps and a hotel. The Path continues close to the sea's edge by Redcliff Point and Black Head to Osmington Mills, where a narrow gorge leads to a rock beach, noted, everyone says, for lobsters. The cliffs are mainly clays and grits. We pass an extensive crop of large masts which occupy the site of the vanished village of Ringstead and so descend to sea level at Ringstead Bay (toll road access).

Now the great chalk cliff of White Nothe rises ahead to over 500ft. The cliff face in between, a National Trust property, is called the Burning Cliff from an incident in 1826, when iron pyrites ignited an outcrop of oil shales which continued to smoulder for the next four years. It is said that the sulphurous vapours were most in evidence at spring tides, from which some connection was inferred between the sea and the ignited materials. We have already noticed a similar phenomenon further west by Charmouth. The Path climbs up and over White Nothe, passing deserted coastguard cottages on the summit, and enters on one of the best sections of Dorset cliff line. Hereabouts there is a very steep way down to the beach.

Half a mile on at West Bottom is a 300ft semi-cylindrical buttress of chalk, which has been called Fountain Rock. The horizontal lines of flints are prominent and there appear to be steep cracks also, which climbers may one day tackle. Near its summit is a stone carrying an inscription to Llewellyn Powys, in fact the local author. The outjutting Bat's Head is holed near sea level; the opening, known as the Eye of the Monster, looks impressive when the setting sun shines through it along the sea. The next bay is dominated by Swyre Head. The limestone, appearing first as a few low reefs—Cow and Calf Rocks and Blind Cow, suddenly produces a fine arch at the eastern extremity of the beach. This is the famous Durdle Door. Heath reports, somewhat surprisingly, that 'a boat could pass through it with all sails set'. It would have to be an exceedingly small craft. The beach is accessible by footpath from the caravan park at the cliff top, but it is probable that traverses of the cliff foot in either direction would present coasteering problems rather beyond the scope of the walker.

Bibliography

O.S. 1 inch Map Sheet 178 (Dorchester)
O.S. 2½ inch Map Sheets SY58, 68, 67, 78, 88
Town Guide from Weymouth
Good, R., *Weyland: the Story of Weymouth and its Countryside*,
    Dorchester, 1945
Nos. 23, 27, 38, 39, 40, 51 from the General Bibliography

22

DURDLE DOOR TO
SOUTH HAVEN POINT

West Lulworth - Worbarrow Bay - Kimmeridge
St Aldhelm's Head - Durlston Head - Swanage
Foreland Point - Studland

THIS outstanding cliff section, the easterly end of considerable importance to rock climbers, also includes, between Lulworth and Kimmeridge, several miles to which access is barred completely by extensive artillery ranges. This is the so-called Isle of Purbeck, never actually an island in the true sense of the word, but a block of high country isolated by Poole Harbour and one-time marshy land along the River Frome.

For the coastal traveller the geological features of the area are for once relatively straightforward. East of Durdle Door the cliffs are in limestone, while the chalk outcrop trends gradually inland forming a range of hills. At Lulworth Cove the sea has breached the limestone wall and chalk forms the back of the bay; further on at Worbarrow Bay the limestone has been removed altogether over a distance of about a mile and a half between Mupe Rocks and Worbarrow Tout, while the chalk ridge is also breached at the Arish Mell gap. Further east the chalk takes the form of a ridge, the Purbeck Hills, some way back from the coastline; the limestone too is isolated in a parallel ridge while the cliffs are of Kimmeridge Clay—alternating shale and stone beds. Between St Aldhelm's Head and Peveril Point the coastline cuts across the outcrop of the Purbeck and Portland limestones which are exposed in steep cliffs. Swanage is in a gap formed in soft rocks between here and the Purbeck Hills which terminate at Ballard Down and Foreland Point in characteristic chalk cliff scenery. Finally Studland Bay round to South Haven Point is once again in newer and softer rocks.

In view of the existence of the range, it is amazing to learn that all this coast lies in the Dorset Area of Outstanding Natural

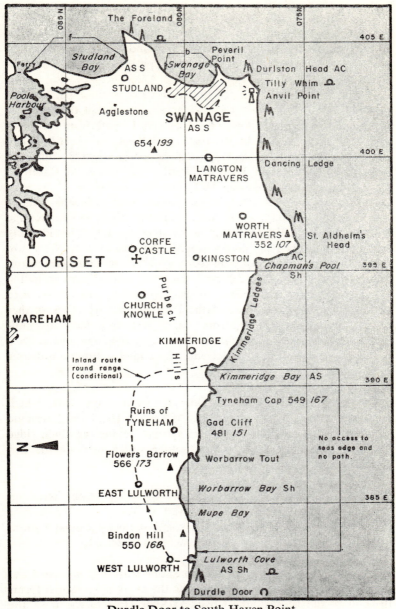

Durdle Door to South Haven Point

(Based upon the Ordnance Survey Map, with the sanction of the Controller of HM
Stationery Office, Crown Copyright reserved)

Beauty. The Tyneham Action Committee is fighting a worthy cause to restore this coastline to our use. Studland Heath is a National Nature Reserve, but there are no coastal properties of the National Trust so far.

By the Path Durdle Door to Lulworth Cove is one mile. Thenceforward 6½ miles of coastline are inaccessible, except that summer visitors are sometimes allowed to Mupe Bay by path from Lulworth and to Worbarrow Bay by the road from West Creech Hill. When they are not firing on the range the detour is about 8½ miles by way of B3070 through West Lulworth, past Lulworth Camp to East Lulworth, up Whiteway Hill and along the ridge of the Purbeck Hills to West Creech Hill, then south through Steeple Village into the valley, through a gap in the limestone ridge to Kimmeridge Village and so to the sea again at Kimmeridge Bay. Should firing be in progress, then the detour would take us almost to Wareham and involve 14 miles mostly on roads. Now on the Path once again, Kimmeridge Bay to St Aldhelm's Head is 5 miles and from the Head to Swanage a further 6 miles. The urban area of Swanage makes a gap of one mile and the Path finishes 6½ miles further on at South Haven Point, from which there is a ferry to Sandbanks and Bournemouth. The total walking distance on the Path is therefore 18½ miles, to which must be added a minimum detour of 8½ miles.

On the cliffs behind Durdle Door the Path is on chalk, which continues round St Oswald's Bay. At Dungy Head the limestone cliffs begin, the coastline turning away and leaving the chalk ridge inland at Hambury Tout. We descend a valley between the two formations to Lulworth Cove.

WEST LULWORTH (SY8280). Access by B3071 from Wool on A352. Nearest station—Wool (4½m). E.C. Weds.
A few hundred yards from the small perfectly-shaped natural harbour of Lulworth Cove. Road access to sea's edge.

The sea has broken through the limestone wall and hollowed out the softer strata behind as far back as the chalk ridge which forms the cliff at the back of the Cove. At Stair Hole to the west, the limestone wall has been similarly breached but the hollowing-out process is not yet far advanced. Nearby are several caves, including Cathedral Cavern, where there are pillars of rock supporting the roof. On the east side of the bay is the famous Fossil Forest. Now there is no longer a path, nor are we permitted to proceed without one.

Let us look first at the coast. Limestone cliffs continue as far as Mupe Rocks (smugglers' cave hereabouts) on the edge of Worbarrow Bay; the chalk ridge behind, Bindon Hill (topped by a promontory Fort), is inland at first but is later cut off to form the sea cliffs at the back of the Bay. The chalk drops to sea level at Arish Mell, rising again immediately beyond the gap to Rings Hill and Flowers Barrow, according to Camden 'a steep and lofty mountain', on which there are the remains of an extensive earthwork. At the eastern side of the Bay the limestone begins again at Worbarrow Tout, a 100ft conical promontory standing ahead of the shoreline. Between here and the chalk the valley of Tyneham Brook has been cut in softer strata of the Wealden Beds. You and I are sometimes permitted to visit Worbarrow, but we must keep to the tracks, the paths, and the beach. Sometimes, when the range is in use, passing ships have to keep fourteen miles clear of the coast! Round the corner are the steep limestone crags of Gad Cliff, running up to 549ft at Tyneham Cap. Sixty years ago Harper faced no such barriers. He describes in those far-off days taking a bicycle along 'the nearest ribbon of sheep-track on the knife edge of the tremendously lofty downs of Broad Bench' with a view of Kimmeridge Bay as would be seen from the car of a balloon. Soon the Kimmeridge Clay begins, forming cliffs of alternating shale and limestone bands, lower but still steep; and so to Kimmeridge Bay where we still have a right to be.

The detour inland forced on us by the range has no comparable scenic attraction, though indeed the road on the summit of the Purbeck Hills commands extensive views, both northward across the Dorset Heaths and south towards the sea.

There is toll road access from Kimmeridge Village to the sea at Kimmeridge Bay. The Path strikes off eastwards along the cliff edge passing a tower on the first hillock. Below at sea level are the horizontal Kimmeridge Ledges which form the floor of the Bay and prevent the waves from reaching the blue-black clay cliffs. The local bituminous shales have been burned in the past by local people as a source of heat and light, as noted for example by Celia Fiennes in her travels in the late seventeenth century. The Path follows the cliff edge below the hill known as Swyre Head (accessible by a toll trackway from Kingston) a fine viewpoint and worth a detour. We descend to a waterfall over low cliffs below Encombe, then climb again over Houns-tout Cliff to Chapman's Pool, a small cove rendered sombre by the dark colours of the Kimmeridge Clay. The cliffs, says Treves, 'are smoke-coloured varying in tint from cinder black to a funeral blue'. This section can be done along the shore at the lowest tide. There is access to Chapman's Pool by a toll road running from Worth Matravers to Kingston; the beach is reached by an easy scramble and there are fossils. Now ahead, jutting out southwards, are the light grey limestones of St Aldhelm's (St Alban's) Head, the beginning of a magnificent stretch of cliffs of Portland and Purbeck Stone which continues eastwards as far as Swanage. We proceed for a time along an undercliff, where in Harper's day 'the paths cunningly led the wayfarer on to morasses formed by the springs oozing from the face of the cliff, to vents and fissures caused by landslips or to fragments of rock as big as houses that had come down from the towered steep'. Eventually by the cliff top we come at over three hundred feet to the Headland, which is surmounted by a small but strongly constructed Norman chapel. This is accessible by a rough trackway from Worth Matravers, which is unmotorable though often motored. The view stretches from the great bulk of Portland to the white cliffs of Wight.

Between St Aldhelm's Head and Durlston Head the Path traces the cliff edge, with steep limestone crags below. This is an important rock climbing area and the passer-by is quite likely to see a climber on the cliff top bringing up his party from the depths; however, so steep are the crags and the slopes of vegetation above them that action views can seldom be had. The first break at Winspit and the second at Seacombe are former quarry areas where there are terraces and caves. Further east we reach the Dancing Ledge, a flat platform just awash at high tide, which is a favourite picnic place and accessible by trackway and footpath from Langton Matravers. Henceforward the cliffs are higher and more continuous, the heart of this new climbing area. A pair of pylons on the cliff top, the first half a mile ahead and the second beyond

Anvil Point, constitute another measured mile used in marine trials. There is a lighthouse at Anvil Point built in 1881, and then come the Tilly Whim Caves, a notable place of pilgrimage (admission charge). It is a former quarry; steps in a tunnel lead from the cliff top to a broad ledge on the cliff face amid fine cliff scenery. Nearby is the well known globe, carved in stone, ten feet in diameter and weighing forty tons (admission charge); the Path passes below it in carefully screened seclusion. The Caves, the Globe, and Durlston Head are all in the grounds of Durlston Castle. We follow straightforward trackways into the urban area of Swanage. Durlston Head is a turning-point from which the coast runs thenceforward northwards; we have views all over Bourne-mouth Bay to the sand cliffs of the mainland and the chalk cliffs of western Wight.

SWANAGE (SZ02/0378/79). Access by A351 from Wareham. BR branch line from Wareham. Youth Hostel. E.C. Thurs.
In 877, a great sea battle took place near here between King Alfred and the Danes. Swanage is mentioned in the Domesday Book. A fishing port in Leland's time, later the centre of the local quarrying industry, now a thriving resort with sandy beach. *See*: Pier; Old Lock-up. *Visit*: Peveril Point; Durlston Head; the Globe; Tilly Whim Caves; Anvil Point Lighthouse; Ballard Down; the Foreland.

The Path begins again at the far end of the front and climbs away along the slopes of Ballard Down, the eastern end of the Purbeck Hill ridge. This is chalk and there are cliffs below and pinnacles offshore, the Haystack and the Pinnacle, 'detached posts and stumps of white rock like a skeleton's lower jaw', as Hardy described it. Two fine caves, known as Parson's Barn (roof over 50ft high) and Little Barn, can be visited by boat. The end of the promontory is called the Foreland, or Handfast Point; offshore the 'Old Harry Rocks' are now much attenuated, in fact little remains of Old Harry's Wife. Harper tells it differently: there were three pinnacles, 'Old Harry, his Wife and Daughter'; Old Harry has gone, his Wife is fading away, while only his Daughter remains! The Path follows the north edge of the promontory round to:

STUDLAND (SZ0382). Access by B3351 from A351 and by minor road from Swanage. Nearest station—Swanage (2½m). Ferry from South Haven Point to Sandbanks. E.C. Thurs.

Pretty village and crowded sandy beach. Treves, sixty years ago, described it as 'a pretty compendium of seaside scenery on a miniature scale', but even then 'a crowd of charabancs and wagonettes crowded its lanes in the summer'. *Visit*: The Agglestone (½m W), an isolated sandstone boulder, 'a crouching monster, brooding upon this amphibious district of sand, bogs and brackish meres'.

There are no more cliffs. The Path traces the flat edge of Studland Bay, reaching in two miles South Haven Point and the ferry to Sandbanks.

Bibliography

O.S. 1 inch Map Sheets 178 (Dorchester) and 179 (Bournemouth)
O.S. 2½ inch Map Sheets SY88, 97, SZ08
Town Guide from Swanage
Anon. *Lulworth: tales of its Witches, Ghosts and Smugglers*, J. Looker Ltd. 1968
Bond, L. M. G., *Tyneham: a lost Heritage*, Dorchester, 1957
Braye, J. (Ed.), *Swanage (Isle of Purbeck)*, 1890
Hardy, W. M., *Old Swanage or Purbeck past and present*, Dorset County Chronicle, 1910
Mansel, J., *Kimmeridge and Smedmore*, 1967
Robinson, C. E., *A Royal Warren (Isle of Purbeck)*, Typographic Etchg Co., 1882
Short, B. C., *The Isle of Purbeck*, 1967
Tatchell, L., *The Heritage of Purbeck*, Dorchester, n.d.
Woodward, I., *In and around the Isle of Purbeck*, 1908
Nos. 23, 27, 38, 39, 40, 51 from the General Bibliography

Appendices

I

WAVES AND TIDES

THE rise and fall of the tides in our oceans is brought about mainly by the moon. While the gravitational attraction between the moon and the waters of the earth is partially responsible for the effect, it is not immediately obvious why there should be high tides, not only beneath the moon, but also on the far side of the earth remote from it. A detailed explanation of this phenomenon is beyond the scope of this book (See Bibliography).

Because of the rotation of the moon about the earth the period between successive tides averages 12hr 25min, the extra 50min per day being required for a particular point on the earth to arrive back immediately beneath the moon. In fact other periodicities in the system make this time variable between 12hr 11min and 12hr 35min. The moon travels round the earth in an elliptical orbit so that the height of the tide increases by some 22% when the moon is nearest (perigee) and decreases by about 16% when it is farthest away (apogee).

The sun also influences the tides; while its mass is considerably greater, its distance is also, so that the overall effect is slightly less than half that of the moon. When the tides due to the sun aid those of the moon, ie at new and full moon, we have spring tides, in between times when they tend to cancel we have neap tides. Spring tides thus occur at fortnightly intervals but due to inertia a day or two after the actual new and full moons. The ratio spring tides/neap tides is 1·46/0·54, ie about 8/3. As the moon's effect is greatest at perigee, the highest tides of all are when perigee falls near new or full moon.

As the orbit of the earth is also elliptical, the tides due to the sun also vary—by about 5%. The sun is at perigee in the winter, so that tides are greater then than at apogee in the summer. In general the sun has the effect of putting the earth's tides slightly out of step with the moon.

The declination of the moon, ie its angular distance above the

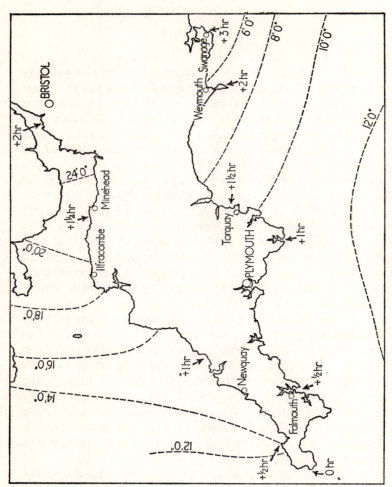

Tide times and tidal ranges in the West Country

equatór, has an important effect on the tides adding a diurnal variation to the semi-diurnal tide. As a result successive tides may be of different heights, though alternate tides are approximately the same. Declination is also responsible for the variations in the tidal interval already mentioned.

We now take a look at what the tides actually do round the West Country coastline. As the tide runs round the world its behaviour in confined waters, such as the English and Bristol Channels, is governed by their orientation and depth and by the shape of the surrounding land. The diagram opposite shows the time of high water along these coasts relative to the time of high tide at Land's End. It is interesting to note that the actual tidal wave travels everywhere in a direction opposite to that of the equilibrium tide. The land mass of Europe blocks direct influence and its effect is only transferred to English waters via the Atlantic Ocean to the west. High water occurs first at Land's End; it is about 1½ hours later at Minehead and about 3hr later at Swanage.

The diagram also shows the variation of tidal range, ie the difference in feet between high and low water marks. The great tidal range of the Bristol Channel, over 20ft at Minehead, is due to resonance for the length and depth of the channel correspond to a resonance condition with a periodicity of about 12hr. A reflected wave travelling back tends to reinforce the next tidal wave travelling forward, and so-called standing waves are set up having a considerable amplitude. In the English Channel the tidal ranges at the ends exceed the value in the middle, around Bournemouth Bay, where it is very small indeed. It is interesting too to note the variation in the western part of the English Channel. The currents associated with the tides are deflected because of the rotation of the earth, the Coriolis Effect; the result in the English Channel is to increase the height of high water on the French coast and the height of low water on the English coast, so that the tidal range is higher on the French side.

A knowledge of tide times and heights is essential for anyone venturing below high water mark. Most coastal resorts and ports display tide times prominently on front or harbour. Otherwise, we work them out beforehand using an almanac which gives tide times for a series of fixed stations and tidal constants to be added or subtracted for places in between. Tidal range data are not so readily come by, but tables are published. The subject is far too complex for this information to be predicted theoretically; it is in fact derived from continuous measurement and extrapolation.

The sea is ever in motion, usually with some pattern of waves passing over its surface layers. We can distinguish two factors which influence waves in the open sea. First, there is swell consisting of waves of fairly long wavelength which have originated, often at a considerable distance, in a violent disturbance or storm and which can travel thousands of miles before their effects become negligible. Secondly, there is the wind which can raise waves when blowing across water even when the surface was initially smooth. The height of such waves depends on the speed of the wind and the distance over which it has acted (known as the fetch). Empirical formulae are as follows:

For storm waves $H = 1 \cdot 5 \sqrt{F}$ (where H is height in feet and F the fetch in miles)

and $H = \dfrac{V^2}{50}$ (where H is the height in feet and V the wind speed in mph)

The relation between height and fetch shows us why the seas are higher in the far west where the fetch can be 3,000 miles for some wind directions. By comparison the fetch in the English or Bristol Channels is only measured in hundreds of miles.

The above considerations apply to waves in deep water. As a wave approaches the shore its behaviour is increasingly influenced by the sea bed, so that when the depth is around half the wavelength we find the velocity almost entirely dependent on the depth. As the waves reach progressively shallower water their velocity diminishes, but the number of waves in a given time stays the same so that the wavelength is diminished; the water tends to pile up and the height of the waves increases. Finally they become unstable and 'break', either by the top sliding down the forward slope (spilling breakers) or by the top overtaking the next trough (plunging breakers). The effects of these on shore erosion are dealt with later. When waves impinge on a breakwater or cliff with deep-water base they are reflected. It is possible for a standing wave to be set up, in a harbour basin for example, but more usually the oncoming and reflected waves interfere to produce a choppy surface.

There are many theories and legends about the periodicity of waves which greatly exceed the average in height—every 7th, every 10th, etc. An arbitrary periodicity may indeed be observable. Even when the process is entirely random it has been estimated that 1 wave in 23 is likely to more than twice the average and 1 in 1,175 more than 3 times the average.

Watching the waves is a never-ending source of enjoyment to the coastal traveller.

Bibliography

Gresswell, R. K., *Beaches and Coastlines*, 1957
Evans, I. O., *Observer's Book of Sea and Seashore*, 1962
Pilkington, R., *The Ways of the Sea*, 1957
Tricker, R. A. R., *Bores, Breakers, Waves and Wakes*, 1964
No. 50 from the General Bibliography

II

THE SHAPE OF THE COASTLINE

THE coastline is moulded by the attacking sea and ceaselessly eroded to a form depending on the type and stratification of the rocks and on the direction of the oncoming waves. These processes were set in train originally by a change in the relative level of land and sea, after which the sea stood relatively higher than before. When a river valley with tributaries is inundated in this way the resulting coastline scenery is known as a ria. There are several examples in the West Country, notably the estuaries of the Fal, the Fowey, the Dart, Plymouth Sound, and so on. Here and there we come across signs of even earlier examples of relative movement of land and sea in the form of raised beaches; east of Prawle Point, for example, the ancient cliffs are separated from the present coastline by the flat platform of a former beach now covered with vegetation; between St Ives and Morvah the coast road runs along a raised beach now some 350ft above sea level.

We have seen in Appendix I how the passing of ocean waves into shallow water causes them to break. A mass of water, known as the swash, runs up the beach until its energy is expended, it then flows back again—the backwash. The swash exerts considerable force on sand or shingle which is hurled up the beach; the backwash has less effect carrying some material back on sandy beaches but often draining back through the stones on a pebble beach. Thus pebble beaches tend to become steeper, while mixed beaches become sorted with the larger material at the top.

When there are about six waves per minute swash and backwash are separate, the above process is unhindered and the waves are said to be constructive. When the frequency is higher each backwash interferes with the following swash and the building-up effect is lessened, so-called destructive waves which result in a net loss of material. When destructive waves beat against an initially sloping coastline, material is removed and a notch is formed marking the farthest point of wave attack. Loose pebbles from the sea floor are hurled against the notch and abraid its lower surface, which eventually wears back far enough for the upper layers to collapse, providing more eroding material. The notch recedes, developing into a cliff, but in the process is subjected less and less

178

to the eroding action of the sea which expends much of its energy on the rock platform at the cliff foot. This platform grows wider as the cliff retreats; sometimes it is obvious as such, mostly it is covered by beach material, sand, or shingle.

The type of cliff which results depends on the nature of the rocks and their dip. Thus when the strata slope inwards the cliff is steep, when they slope outwards upper layers tend to slide over lower and produce areas of landslip. Chalk, relatively soft and not markedly stratified, erodes steadily into very steep cliffs, while granite, hard and jointed, produces the characteristic castellated effect. When the cliff rocks are mixed wave action is of course more violent on the softer parts and inlets (called zawns in Cornwall), caves, etc, can be formed depending on the exact arrangement of the strata. The collapse of a cave at the inward end produces a funnel hole or blow hole, of which there are many West Country examples.

When waves approach a shoreline with oblique incidence, the slowing down as shallow water is reached results in a bending of the wave front towards the shore (the well known phenomenon of refraction, familiar when we look at objects below the surface of water). Similarly when waves approach an indented shoreline the refraction results in their lapping round headlands which are attacked from the sides; similarly in bays the attack is directed to the sides and away from the centre. This wave behaviour tends to emphasise the form of a promontory; first, if the strata are suitably disposed, a cave is formed; this is followed by an arch through the promontory and finally, when this collapses, an offshore stack is produced. By the same argument an offshore island is subject to wave attack all round and not just on its seaward face. We reach, too, some inkling of why the beach material in a bay is sometimes arranged with the smallest at the sides and the largest in the middle; on the other hand continuous gradation in size over long distances, as at Chesil Beach, is not yet fully understood.

A wave approaching the beach obliquely (it is clear from Appendix I, *Waves and Tides*, that this is often the case in the West Country) drives the swash obliquely up the slope. The backwash on the other hand runs neither directly down the beach nor back in the direction of incidence, but onwards at an angle as though the wave had been reflected on impact. As a result solid materials borne by the waves are carried slowly along the beach away from the direction of incidence. In this way pebbles are moved for many miles along the coastline, eg in the English Channel from the pebble beds of Budleigh Salterton even as far as Dungeness. Longshore drift, we say, is from west to east. In places local conditions force the sea to deposit much of the transported material in one place; a bank of shingle (or sand) is built up in places over a length of many miles. Local conditions can produce a shingle spit in a direction the reverse of the main longshore drift, as for example at the Den, Teignmouth.

Longshore transport tends to denude resorts of their beach material and, to combat this, the local authorities build groynes—wooden fences running at right angles to the sea from above high water to below low water. Transported material builds on the up-drift side of the groynes and stays there. However, the building of groynes at one place may increase erosion down-drift, more groynes have to be built there and so the process goes on.

Sometimes the headlands are of harder rocks than the bays between, as for example at Woolacombe and Swanage. In some places it is just local strengthening by veins of harder material which enables the headlands to resist. In any case headlands are subject to much sterner attack by the sea, often at all states of the tide; their destruction is inevitable, the material being continuously transferred to the bays between or along. The effect in the long term is to straighten the coastline into gently curving lines, as at Seaton.

Often when conditions are appropriate beach sand is blown inland by the wind to form extensive dune areas, such as Braunton Burrows, Perran Sands, etc. Movement and incursion of dunes can be controlled by the planting of suitable vegetation, such as marram grass. Sometimes a great storm will remove all the loose beach material in a cove, eliminating sand and leaving rock or even the basal rock platform. Continuing deposition sooner or later reverts conditions to something approaching normal, though indeed long period fluctuations between rock and sand are known to occur.

The sea exerts tremendous forces on the coastline. The spectacular results provide continuous entertainment for the coastwise traveller.

Bibliography
See Appendix I

III

ROCKS, MINERALS, AND MINING

THE counties of Devon and Cornwall and that part of Somerset threaded by the Path consist of old resistant rocks of the Devonian and Carboniferous periods (with some even older at Lizard, Bolt Head, and Start Point) arranged in broad bands trending from east to west. In the so-called Armorican folding in Permo-Carboniferous times these south-western rocks were thrust towards the resistant block of Wales to the north, muds and shales were hardened and the strata fantastically contorted. The best examples of this are seen between Hartland Point and Dizzard Point. The whole forms a huge anticline with the older Devonian rocks between Minehead and Barnstaple and from Boscastle right round to Torbay sandwiching the newer Carboniferous beds which appear at the coast between Barnstaple and Boscastle.

Then, during Carboniferous times, huge masses of magma were injected from below, baking and altering the surrounding rocks to form a slaty material often called killas. As the mass cooled granite-forming minerals—felspar, quartz, and mica—crystallised out, while other volatile materials separated as liquids or gases to form metalliferous ore-bearing veins. Boron replaced the mica in some of the granite to form tourmaline, fluorine produced certain characteristic minerals and carbonic acid in places converted the felspar to kaolinite, the future basis of the china-clay industry. Finally, much later on, erosion exposed some of these granite masses at the surface.

The metalliferous ore bearing zones are arranged in a series round the granite mass, characterised by the temperature of crystallisation. Thus closest to the granite are tin oxide (cassiterite) and tungsten minerals; then follow the sulphide source of copper with minerals of nickel, cobalt and arsenic. The third zone is one of zinc and lead sulphides, and finally in the fourth zone come iron minerals. This explains why certain mines, eg Levant, dug originally for copper were later turned over to tin production by sinking the shafts even deeper.

Tin mining goes back to the earliest times, for it is likely that Cornwall was the site of the legendary Cassiterides where the Phoenicians came to trade for the metal some 3,500 years ago.

For a long time tin was obtained by streaming, that is from rocks eroded naturally by streams, or below sea cliffs. Lode mining began early in the seventeenth century and henceforward the over-riding problem of mining became increasingly that of removing water from the workings. Many miles of drainage tunnels (adits) were bored. Manpower, horse-power and water-wheels were used, all had their limitations, until finally the advent of the steam engine enabled the miners to go deep enough for full exploitation of the lodes. The Newcomen engine led the way early in the eighteenth century, then fifty years later came the more efficient Watt engine. Soon every mine had its engine house and chimney stack and it is the ruins of these buildings in particular which make the characteristic landscape of these mining areas today.

For about one hundred years from the mid-eighteenth to the mid-nineteenth century the mining of copper was more important than that of tin. Indeed, in the early 1800s, Cornwall was the principal world source of copper and several of her smaller ports were founded originally for its export. However in later years alternative and more accessible sources were discovered overseas, so that by 1865 tin came to the fore once again. In many places, as we have said, fresh sources of tin were discovered below the copper and the almost defunct mines blossomed forth again into the new trade. Tin mining continued to flourish until World War I, but subsequently it declined so that after World War II only two active mines remained, at Geevor near St Just and South Crofty near Camborne. During the last decade they have been taking another look in various places, other mines have reopened for a time and there is some possibility that the industry may start to increase once again. The effect on the scenery can only be deleterious, for while the former relics have by now been largely absorbed into the landscape, modern industrial despoliation is considerably more efficient.

For the traveller on the Path all the extensive remains of former mining are industrial archaeological sites. Some mines and adits can still be explored by anyone willing to undertake the serious personal risk (some enthusiastic cavers have indeed turned to mines because of the shortage of natural holes in this part of England). Care is needed among the buildings which totter slowly but definitely; the dangers of shafts, some completely open, some choked at the surface, are obvious and they are usually efficiently fenced. The spoil heaps may still be a source of mineral specimens, natural crystals, and so on. The casual passer-by is hardly likely to be rewarded—too many others have gone before; equipment and diligent searching are usually required. Every aspect is well documented now, and there are museums at Penzance, Camborne, and Truro.

East of Torbay the Path moves on to newer rocks. First comes the New Red Sandstone of the Permian and Trias periods, which forms the characteristic red rocks and earth of Devon and stretches on past Dawlish and Exmouth to Sidmouth. At Seaton we reach even newer Lias formations, blue and yellow limestones and shales with a capping of Cretaceous rocks, chalk and Greensand. Beer Head is the first chalk headland. Beyond Burton Bradstock the mighty Chesil Beach, made of flints from the chalk and quartzite from the New Red Sandstone, leads on to a great mass of Jurassic limestone, the Isle of Portland. Beyond Weymouth a chalk ridge sweeping down from Salisbury Plain and Cranborne Chase runs parallel to the coast as the Purbeck Hills finally reaching the sea at the Foreland, Swanage. South of it a limestone ridge gradually develops from the sea, fragmentary at first then forming substantial cliffs by Lulworth. Beyond Worbarrow Bay this limestone continues to St Aldhelm's Head and by more fine cliffs to Durlston Head. The last few miles of the Path are on the sandy heathlands of the Tertiary formations of the Hampshire Basin.

Pebble collecting on beaches was once a very popular pastime. It is said that the careful searcher may still discover semi-precious stones such as amethyst, citrine, chalcedony, agate, carnelian, jasper, and so forth. This may be, but there is pleasure as well in hunting for sea-polished specimens from the various coloured rocks which are passed along the route of the Path. These can be made into unusual and quite attractive items of jewellery in suitable settings. Mineral specimens can often be obtained on beaches where the lodes in the cliff face have been eroded by the sea. Fossils are similarly exposed; indeed the Lias area of Dorset is an outstanding fossil hunting-ground.

Bibliography

Barton, D. B., *A Guide to the Mines of West Cornwall*, Truro, 1965

Barton, R. M., *An Introduction to the Geology of Cornwall*, Truro, 1964
idem, *Cornwall's Structure and Scenery*, Truro, 1969
Borner, R., *Minerals, Rocks and Gemstones*, Edinburgh, 1967
Davies, G. M. *The Dorset Coast–a Geological Guide*, 1956
Ellis, C., *The Pebbles on the Beach*, 1954
Ferris, L. C., *Pebbles on Cornwall's Beaches*, Truro, 1969
Hamilton-Jenkin, A. K., *The Cornish Miner*, 1962
Ordish, H. G., *Cornish Engine Houses*, Truro, 1967
idem, *Cornwall's Structure and Scenery*, Truro, 1969
   1968
Rogers, C., *A Collector's Guide to Minerals, Rocks and Gemstones in Cornwall and Devon*, Truro, 1969
Williams, H. V., *Cornwall's Old Mines*, Truro, 1969
Nos. 2 and 49 from the General Bibliography

IV

WILD FLOWERS

This appendix is intended to help walkers to recognise wild flowers which they may encounter while traversing the Path. Considerations of space confine it to plants which are to some extent unusual, or at any rate are not as common as daisies. It is not compiled in any scientific order and makes no attempt to cater for botanists, who after all can look after themselves. Those who wish to see what the flowers actually look like should consult the books listed in the bibliography.

Generally speaking, most of the plants have a fairly wide range along the coast, so the localities where they grow are not indicated unless there is some special reason for doing so. Some areas such as Berry Head (limestone) and the Lizard (serpentine) have plants specially suited to their type of soil.

Samphire *(Crithmum maritimum)* is almost entirely confined to the cliffs. It has juicy stems and leaves which are aromatic when crushed. Boiled in vinegar it was used for pickles in the Middle Ages, the gathering of it being referred to in King Lear as a 'dreadful trade'.

Scurvy Grass *(Cochlearia officinalis)* is about the first coastal plant to bloom (April). It has dense masses of snowy white flowers, the leaves being roughly heart-shaped and purplish underneath. It contains an oil with anti-scorbutic properties and was often used as a remedy for scurvy by seamen—it is mentioned in Captain Cook's diaries. Another variety *(C. anglica)* is abundant on salt marshes like those at Newquay.

Squill *(Scilla)*. There are two varieties of this which look much alike. They are both beautiful little lilac flowers, with narrow leaves, which grow from bulbs and are profuse in localities which they favour. *S. verna* blooms in the spring and grows in West Penwith, whereas *S. autumnalis* comes out in August and September on the North Cornwall coast and at the Lizard. In the old days a syrup was extracted from the bulbs and used as a cough cure, but it was said to be 'bitter, strong and most unpleasant'.

Burnet Rose *(Rosa spinosissima)*. This is usually found in a low-growing tangle of scrub on the cliff top and as the name implies, the creeping stems are covered with a mass of small prickles. The small flowers are out from May to September and are white or pink.

Tree Mallow *(Lavatera arborea)*. Perhaps the most beautiful of the seaside plants with pale purple flowers over an inch across from July to September. It grows up to 5 feet high, with large leaves on long stalks, and is also to be found at places inland because in the old days it was used for compounding poultices and ointments.

Triangular-stalked Garlic *(Allium triquetrum)*. This grows in the Land's End area and looks like a white bluebell at first sight. However the triangular flower stem and the characteristic smell soon show the difference. It is not native to Britain, having come across from France, and in the Channel Islands is classified as a noxious weed.

Warren Crocus *(Romulea columnae)*. A beautiful little plant, growing from a bulb and with a pale lilac flower. It is to be found in April on Dawlish Warren and very occasionally elsewhere.

Mesembryanthemum *(Carpobrotus edulis)*. A South African plant, where it has an edible fruit, hence its English name of Hottentot Fig. It has spread from gardens and is now firmly established on cliffs and sea walls on the southern coast of Devon and Cornwall. It is thick and fleshy and usually trails downwards in mats. The flowers are a garish magenta, occasionally yellow.

Sea carrot *(Daucus gingidium)*. Quite common in the South West and closely resembling the Wild Carrot *(D. carota)*. They are possibly natives of southern Europe but of very ancient cultivation in England. In the former the flower umbels are flat or convex whereas in the latter they are concave, but there are many cross-pollinated forms. The buds are pink, but most of the flowers come out white. They can be identified by the very marked involucre below the umbel and by the carroty smell of the root.

Lesser Dodder *(Cuscuta epithymum)*. A plant which is parasitic on gorse and heather. It has a mass of reddish coloured twining thread-like stems which attach themselves to the host plant by minute suckers but have no roots in the earth. The flowers, pale pink in colour, are individually very small but grow close together in globular form.

Montbretia. This plant is an escape from gardens, but it is

naturalised in many places in Cornwall, usually in damp ditches where its bright yellow-orange flowers are very showy.

Henbane *(Hyoscyamnus niger)*. Found in a few places, for instance near Mawnan, Hayle, and Bigbury. It is a foot or two high with rather large leaves and short-stalked dingy yellow flowers with purple veins. It has an unpleasant smell and is poisonous, as it contains hyoscine, which was used by the notorious Dr Crippen.

Portland Spurge *(Euphorbia portlandica)*. A low-growing plant with fleshy leaves and milky juice. The flower heads are small, cup-shaped and greenish in colour. As its name indicates it grows on Portland Bill but it is also to be found elsewhere.

Sea Pea *(Lathyrus japonicus)*. A small plant of the usual pea form with purplish flowers, which only grows on a few shingle beaches, notably Chesil Beach.

Wild Cabbage *(Brassica oleracea)*. A large handsome plant with broad leaves and yellow flowers in a tall spike, which grows on the Dorset coast and near Fowey and Polruan. It is the wild parent from which were derived the garden cabbages, brussels sprouts and broccoli.

Large Lizard Clover *(Trifolium molinerii)*. Though called 'large', it is actually a rather small plant with yellow flowers of the usual clover shape. It is native to Britain but in fact only grows near the Lizard and in the Channel Islands, even though it is common on the Continent.

Bibliography

Hepburn, I. *Flowers of the Coast*, 1952
Keble, Martin, *Concise British Flora in Colour*, 1969
Nicholson, B. E., Ary S. and Gregory M., *The Oxford Book of Wild Flowers*, 1960
Paton, J., *Flowers of the Cornish Coast*, Truro, n.d.
idem, *Wild Flowers in Cornwall*, Truro, 1968
Skene, MacGregor, *A Flower Book for the Pocket*, 1952

V

BIRDS

ALL the users of the coastal path, whether they have ornithological interests or just a general interest in the countryside, are bound to be struck by the tremendous variety of the bird life—the wide range of woodland, moorland, and sea birds.

The Raven, the largest member of the crow family, may be seen flying and indulging in aerial manœuvres at all seasons of the year—unmistakeable in size, shape, and voice. It is also our earliest breeding bird, often having eggs as early as February in its nest high on a sea cliff.

The Common Buzzard, a rare bird in most parts of the country, is fortunately still frequently seen in the West Country, soaring on broad eagle-shaped wings over moorland or cliff as it circles effortlessly in the warm air.

With the dashing Peregrine Falcon the situation is similar to so many rare birds, it is fighting for survival and deserves all the protection we can afford it. They are only likely to be seen along the more inaccessible parts of the coast. Another bird of prey, the Kestrel, is quite common at all seasons of the year and can be watched as it hovers facing into the wind, searching for its prey chiefly small rodents.

The Sparrow Hawk, although approximately the same size as the Kestrel, is hardly likely to be confused with it as its method of hunting is completely different. It is a darker bird with shorter wings and a longer tail, but you will probably only get a fleeting view as it dashes over the next hedgerow. It is seldom seen flying at any great height.

Where the Path wanders along wooded cliff slopes such birds as the Carrion Crow, the Magpie, and the more colourful Jay dominate the scene, while the cheeky Jackdaws descend over the cliff sides like falling leaves. The Woodpigeon is common everywhere and the Blue Rock Dove is found sparingly along the coast, also the dainty Turtle Dove, one of our summer migrants conspicuous by the white border to the tail which it often displays.

The high moor which runs almost to the cliff top in certain areas has its own particular attraction. It is often the breeding haunt of the Curlew, the largest of our waders—with a wild whistling call and long down-curved bill, it is easily identified. The Lapwing, our most common Plover, will be found in similar situations, often in company with Golden Plover.

Where the Path wends over lower-lying land, especially the estuaries, large flocks of Oystercatchers, conspicuous in their pied plumage, with brilliant red bill and orange legs, can often be approached to within a few yards. Feeding with them will often be the Ringed Plover and Common Sandpiper. Occasionally a Snipe might be disturbed, and as one journeys west into Cornwall the Turnstone becomes quite a common bird; it, too, is very tame as it feeds in the seaweed and marine débris on the shore and in the harbours.

The Chaffinch is common everywhere, so also is the Bullfinch, causing at times concern to the gardener. The Greenfinch is not seen so frequently.

Of the Buntings the Common Yellow Bunting, known popularly as the Yellow Hammer, is easily the most numerous; Reed Buntings are found in suitable places, and West Cornwall is a likely place to see the Snow Bunting when on migration in the autumn and spring. It is also late in the autumn when we see our own flocks of Redwings and Fieldfares, visiting us once again from the northern countries.

It is in the sheltered wooded valleys that we hear the Green Woodpecker calling. If we rest awhile here we might see the Nuthatch and the Tree Creeper searching for food in the bark of a nearby tree. By the side of the swiftly flowing stream the intriguing Dipper might be watched, looking like a large dark Wren with a white breast, his lovely song mingling with the sound of the water.

The brilliantly coloured Kingfisher is now rare, but the fortunate watcher may see one. One of the most striking birds seen fishing in the smallest stream or on a wide estuary is the tall Heron, still fairly common in Devon and Cornwall.

During the spring and summer months the scimitar-shaped Swift, the long forked-tailed Swallow, the white-rumped House Martin and the shorter-tailed Sand Martin are flying all day long until dusk, feeding whilst on the wing.

The more experienced ornithologist will find the West Country rich in the variety of Warblers. There are the Dartford, Chiffchaff, Willow Warbler, White-throat, Reed Warbler, Sedge Warbler; the Nightingale is seldom found as far west as Devon and Cornwall.

On the various ponds and reservoirs the species of birds will vary at different seasons of the year, and often winter is the most rewarding time. To be seen then are Coots, Moorhens, Little Grebes, Mute Swans, Mallard, Teal, Wigeon, Shoveller, to mention a few of the more common ones.

In the estuaries and just off the shore in winter, numbers of the lovely Shelduck are widely distributed, also the Goldeneye, Common Scoter, Eider-duck, Tufted-duck, and large numbers of Wigeon, mixed with Mallard, and Teal.

A really cold spell will often bring wild geese to the West Country, the small Black Brent, the Whitefronted, the larger Canada and a few Grey Lags. With the exception of the Canada geese, they are usually very shy and it is difficult to approach them closely.

As would be expected on a coastal walk, seabirds will be observed in abundance and variety. Of our six species of British Gull, five breed in the West Country, the most numerous and widely distributed being the Herring Gull—the large gull that frequents the harbours and sea fronts. The Lesser Black Backed Gull, similar in size, is comparatively uncommon. The largest British gull, the Greater Black Backed Gull, is well distributed throughout the west and large gatherings can be seen at times on Enys Dodnan, a rocky stack near Land's End.

On suitable parts of the Cornish coast Kittiwakes breed in very compact colonies. It is a dainty little gull, its dark eye giving it a rather gentle appearance. Black-headed Gulls, approximately the same size as the Kittiwake, are easily distinguished by their red bill and legs and the black head that adorns them in spring and summer only.

Along the sandy shores and low parts of the coastline the swallow-like Terns may be watched as they dive for fish in the shallows. It is not easy to differentiate betwen the Arctic and Common Terns as both have red legs and bill, but the larger Sandwich Tern with its dark bill, and also the Little Tern, are easily identified.

A family of sea birds known as Auks have their breeding colonies on the more precipitous sea cliffs. It is only during the breeding season that these birds ever come ashore voluntarily. Identification of the three species is straightforward; the Guillemot has a sharp dagger-like bill and on the breeding ledges they pack as closely as they can stand; the Razorbill has a much heavier bill and its plumage is several shades darker; the Puffin is shorter in the body than the others and has a short multi-coloured bill, which gives it a rather comical expression.

One of the most interesting and remarkable events in modern ornithology has been the increase in the Fulmar Petrel as a breeding species. Over a hundred years ago it bred only on St Kilda and other remote Scottish islands. Then the bird started to extend its breeding range and colonised the mainland sea cliffs in Scotland at the turn of the century; it continued southwards, until in 1956 it commenced to breed on the North Devon cliffs. It now breeds all the way down to Land's End. The Fulmar is a truly marine bird, only coming to the cliffs at breeding time. The one white egg is laid late in May and the bird remains on the cliffs until early September. The adult bears a superficial resemblance to the Gull, but its narrow straight wings, fast gliding flight and large black eyes make identification certain. On closer inspection the Petrel bill with the tubular nostrils is observed.

The other large sea birds that breed along the cliffs and are with us all the year are the Cormorant and its slightly smaller relative the Shag. These birds are found in similar localities. The Shag lacks the white patches that the Cormorant has on the throat and thighs; both species can often be watched from the cliff as they are fishing.

The largest and our most spectacular sea bird is the Gannet. At all times of the year Gannets can be watched as they dive for fish, often from a considerable height; they no longer breed on Lundy, but are almost sure to be seen off the coast of West Penwith.

Perhaps it would be appropriate to remark in conclusion that the Adder, our only venomous snake, is fairly common on cliff paths. It varies tremendously in colour, being all shades from golden to black. It is, however, very timid and will make off if disturbed, the only danger arising if it is stepped upon accidentally.

Bibliography

Fisher, J., *Bird Recognition Vol. 1–Sea-birds and Waders*, 1947
Fisher, J. and Lockley, R. M., *Sea Birds*, 1954
Lockley, R. M., *Birds of the Sea*, 1945
Moore, R., *The Birds of Devon*, Newton Abbot, 1969
Penhallurick, R. D., *Birds of Cornwall–Sea and Shore*, Truro, 1970
idem, *Birds of the Cornish Coast*, Truro, 1970
No. 50 from the General Bibliography

VI

SEA-SHORE LIFE

FORTUNATELY the West Country is very rich in the variety of its seashore life, with hundreds of miles of coastline, facing the Bristol Channel in the north, the Atlantic Ocean on the west, and the English Channel along the south.

This appendix is for the guidance of the walker, coasteer and country-lover in general and is not meant to be a comprehensive guide for the serious naturalist. Nevertheless it is hoped that these notes will draw attention to some of the interesting things along the shore that might otherwise pass unnoticed.

On the western seaboard there is an abundance of rocky and boulder-strewn beaches, as well as many miles of sandy shore. It is on the former, in pools both deep and shallow, that the more inquisitive searcher will be amply rewarded. Low water is the ideal time, that is from approximately two hours before low tide until, perhaps, two hours after the tide has turned. It is necessary to insert a word of caution here. On many beaches in the west it is possible to be cut off by the incoming tide, so however interesting the beach and its life may be a watchful eye has to be kept on the time and the tide. Every year the local papers publish accounts of visitors being rescued from isolated beaches, but it is probably wise to avoid involvement with expensive rescue proceedings. In most cases it would be safe to sit tight out of reach of the sea until the tide went down again, although in the meantime someone might turn up and insist on a rescue.

Crustaceans have probably been familiar to most of us since childhood, and catching shrimps and prawns can still be an absorbing pastime. They are found in most pools at low tide.

In some of the more sheltered rocky inlets and bays at low water the Edible Crab may be found in holes and recesses in the rocks. Specimens may weigh up to two pounds. It is easily distinguishable from the Common Rock Crab and the Velvet Fiddler, being a reddish brown, while the other two are a very dark green in colour. The Edible Crab is very slow in movement compared with the other two, and usually possesses a much larger pair of claws.

Although another species of crab, the Thorny Spider Crab, is the same colour as the Edible, it is not possible to confuse it with the others because of its long spidery legs, thorny shell and very insignificant claws. Lobsters are more rarely seen; an eight-inch length is considered the minimum and anything smaller should not be taken. The small Squat Lobster may be found by diligent searching; it is too small to be edible but is a very attractive little creature. A small shell seen moving along the bottom of a pool is likely to be the adopted home of one of the several species of Hermit Crab.

On the rocky shores in the smallest of pools will almost certainly be found some species of the lovely Sea anemones. These flower-like creatures are really animals and feed on shrimps, sand hoppers and any small fry that they can attract. They paralyse their victims with poison from their tentacles and then digest them at leisure. There are over seventy species of Sea anemone on the British list and it is probable that more than half this number will be found in the area covered by this book. The smooth anemone is the most common—it varies in colour and can be dark crimson, olive green, or brown. When the tentacles are expanded a ring of bead-like objects of a bright blue colour is revealed, which gives it one of its local names of 'Beadlet'.

Jelly fish appear around the coast in vast numbers usually after a period of fine settled weather and calm seas, when the conditions suit them. Occasionally large ones are found washed up on the shore. A species named the Marigold is by far the most common and can be identified by four crimson rings on its body. Like all jelly fish it has the power to sting on contact and on a person with a sensitive skin it will cause a reaction in the form of nettle rash.

The largest number of species come under the heading of Molluscs (Shellfish) and it is certain that we cannot walk on any beach without stopping to admire and wonder at the vast variety of the sea shells.

In this group are some fish that are rather more interesting than attractive—the Cuttle fish, the Squid and the Octopus. The remains of the Cuttle fish are more often found than the living fish; the shell is white, fairly flat and oval in shape. It is often collected for caged birds. The Squid and Octopus are only likely to be found in the deeper rock pools. Both can swim and crawl and, when alarmed, they move rapidly by discharging a jet of water through an organ known as a syphon; they can also discharge a dark inky fluid to confuse pursuers.

Two of the most common shell fish are Limpets and Mussels, found almost everywhere attached to rocks below the high tide mark, the mussels sometimes in incredibly dense clusters. Cockles are more numerous on the sandy beaches and can be dug for in suitable places—sandy estuaries are favourite breeding sites. Winkles are common and again edible. The Dog Winkle, which is slightly larger and dark purple in colour, although not poisonous, is gritty inside and unpleasant to eat.

The coastal path walker, however, may not have the time or the inclination to collect edible shell-fish. Even so he may still take an interest in the empty shells found lying on the beaches. The dainty cowry is often found in fine shingle, together with other small ornamental shells such as the Wentletrap, the Sting Winkle and the beautifully coloured, cone-shaped Painted Top. Occasionally the large, flat, fan-shaped shell of the Scallop can be picked up— the larger ones are often sold in souvenir shops as ashtrays. In fact the sale of sea shells is booming and large specimens can now be bought at many seaside places.

Although not seen in great numbers, seals are not uncommon round the coast of West Penwith. The walker here will be unfortunate if he fails to spot the Atlantic Grey Seal sporting in the breakers along the rocky coast or sunning on the wave platforms of stacks or reefs. The smaller Common Seal, which will also be seen occasionally, appears to have wider distribution. The writer once saw one toying with a large fish close to the rocks off Baggy Point in North Devon. At the same place on more than one occasion we have watched a school of porpoises sporting themselves as they swam by only a quarter of a mile offshore. Sharks appear, and are caught, off the south coast of Cornwall.

Of the various kinds of seaweeds there is a great variety. Perhaps the most interesting is that known as laver, which is often collected from the rocks at low tide by local folk. It is much esteemed as a food, being thoroughly washed to remove the fine grains of sand and then boiled for a considerable time with added vinegar. In its natural form on the rocks it is a dark green transparent substance the thickness of brown paper. It also has medicinal uses.

M*

Bibliography

Barrett, J. and Yonge, C. M., *Collins Pocket Guide to the Sea Shore*, 1958
Evans, I. O., *Observer's Book of Sea and Seashore*, 1962
Ingle, R., *A Guide to the Seashore*, 1969
Matthews, G. and Parks, P., *Seashore Life*, 1965
Pascoe, A., *Sea Shells on Cornwall's Beaches*, Truro, n.d.
Turk, S. M., *Seashore Life in Cornwall*, Truro, 1970
Yonge, C. M., *The Sea Shore*, 1966
No. 50 from the General Bibliography

VII

COASTEERING

COASTEERING is to coastlines what mountaineering is to mountains. It embraces a similar range of activities from the gentlest of walking on the easiest of slopes to the hardest of rock climbing on crags vertical or even more so. The cliff-top walk parallels the mountain-ridge walk, the cliff climb the mountain-crag climb, the ascent of stacks, pinnacles, and islands the surmounting of virgin summits, the traverse of a beach the traverse of a mountain. Much the same techniques are employed, though problems of snow and ice only occur on high mountains and problems of sailing and swimming only by the sea. The coasteer probably enjoys better weather, but in any case is in much lesser danger if it changes. They both encounter the elemental forces of Nature on a huge scale. The mountaineer climbs eventually away from life to a place where there is only ice, snow, and rock, the coasteer seldom leaves the rich flora and fauna of the sea and sea-level land. The coasteer never knows the really high endeavour of the mountaineer, but then such deeds are not for everyone.

The terrain of the coasteer lies between the edge of cultivation and the offshore point where the sea remains more or less unbroken at all states of the tide. In between, for his entertainment, lie the following—the cliff top (walking here is the main subject of this book); the cliff (where there may be crags for climbers); the shore, the area between low water mark and the cliff foot which is divided into backshore above high water mark and foreshore below it (often walking territory, but there may also be pinnacles to climb, while sometimes it is difficult, or even impossible, to progress from one 'easy way down' to the next between the tides); offshore (where there may be pinnacles or stacks needing a boat or a swim for access). There may be caves to explore in any of the above. It is with this terrain and with these features of it that the coasteer concerns himself.

Now for the extra things the coasteer has to do! Sometimes he will need a boat for access as was used to reach the big stacks of St Kilda, the bulky pinnacle of the highest of the Needles off the Isle of Wight and the Sugarloaf on the Isle of Man. Similar tactics would certainly be called for in the West Country, for some of the sea stacks and to reach caves in deep-water cliffs. The walker on a flat coast might carry a light collapsible boat in order to escape long detours to bridges; he would save many miles for example by crossing the mouth of the Taw-Torridge in this way from Braunton Burrows to the Popple at Westward Ho! Proficiency in handling the boat would be essential. Sometimes a swim would serve the same purpose, but this necessity is most likely to arise in the course of a cliff traverse for, when confronted by a steep-sided cleft going down into deep water, swimming is the only way, at least for the first man. He can perhaps construct an aerial ropeway for the rest. Wading, paddling and the use of holds below the water are also involved; in fact, where does climbing stop?

Sometimes the coasteer is cut off by loose, vegetation-covered or otherwise impassable cliff from pinnacles on the beach in every way worthy of his attention. In this case he is permitted to use a rope ladder, which is much more suitable for this particular job than any method of descending or ascending on the climbing rope itself. He has also on cliff sides and tops to work his way through very dense vegetation. Secateurs are helpful, also gloves, and perhaps a kukri would not be amiss. This vegetation and its thorns provide the main incentive for the wearing of climbing boots rather than plimsolls, which are suitable for most other aspects of coast work, and of long trousers rather than shorts.

The handling of smooth sea-worn rocks covered by the more slimy varieties of seaweed is another awkward problem. One of the pioneers claimed to solve it by what he called 'touch and pass' —the boulder hopper did not stop long enough in one place to fall over, but even this requires a great deal of balance control. Another recommended an alpenstock, but this might well produce more problems than it solved.

Cliff climbing was first carried out for purely utilitarian reasons. Shakespeare in *King Lear* describes the collecting of samphire from the chalk faces at Dover; local people descended the cliffs near Combe Martin and elsewhere in search of laver. In St Kilda a hundred years ago the hardy inhabitants climbed the steep walls of the stacks for birds and their eggs; so important was this skill that the young ladies are said to have picked a marriage partner above all else for his climbing ability. The first sporting climbs on cliffs were made by R. M. Barrington in the 1880s when he persuaded the St Kildans to show him their route on Stac na Biorrach, an expedition which he described subsequently in the *Alpine Journal*. Coasteering began in the West Country around the turn of the century when Tom Longstaff, later a noted mountaineer, climbed at Bull Point and on Lundy. A few years later Arthur Andrews, already an experienced climber on British rocks, went to live near Zennor and it was his enthusiasm and energy through the years which established the advanced climbing school of West Penwith. We must also notice E. A. N. Arber, a geologist, who first suggested the idea of beach traverses of great length in North Devon and Clement Archer and Cecil Agar, who carried them out in the 1950s. The principal climbing areas are Lynmouth to Bull Point, Clovelly to Widemouth, West Penwith, Berry Head, Torquay Harbour to Petit Tor Point and St Aldhelm's Head to Durlston Head, but tremendous scope remains everywhere.

The walker on the Path may well see climbers in action, particularly at Bosigran (Chapter 9), Chair Ladder (Chapter 10), Torbay (Chapter 17) and East Dorset (Chapter 22). He may decide to participate in a minor way by climbing the odd wall of rock beside the route or scrambling on the easier foreshore pinnacles, undoubtedly enriching his experience in the process. But steep crags, high crags, exposed crags and traverses close to the sea are for experts only.

Bibliography

Andrews, A. W. and Pyatt, E. C., *Cornwall*, Climbers' Club, 1950
Annette, B., *Limestone Climbs on the Dorset Coast*, Cade, n.d.
Archer, C. H., *Coastal Climbs in North Devon (with supplements)*. Privately, 1961–65
Biven, P. H. and McDermott, M. B., *Cornwall Vol. 1 North Coast of West Penwith*, Climbers' Club, 1968
Exeter C.C., *Torbay Climbing Guide* (in the press)
Moulton, R.D., *Lundy Rock Climbs*, R.N. Mountaineering Club, 1970
Moulton, R. D. (Ed.), *Rock Climbing in Devonshire*, R.N. Mountaineering Club, 1966
Stevenson, V. N., *Cornwall Vol. 2 West and South Coasts of West Penwith*, Climbers' Club, 1966
White, R. C. (Ed.), *Dorset*, Climbers' Club, 1969
No. 39 from General Bibliography

VIII

ISLANDS

WE define an island, strictly an offshore island, as land surrounded by water at all states of the tide; we concede perhaps the title also to land surrounded at high tide but joined to an adjacent larger land mass at low tide, and call it a foreshore island. When small in area, islands become islets. When the height begins to approach the dimensions of the base, and certainly when it exceeds them, we use the terms stack or pinnacle, again with the defining adjectives, offshore and foreshore, to denote the location. A rock submerged at high tide is no longer an island but a reef.

Islands provide sites in miniature for cliff top and beach walking, in fact for the whole range of activities which is coasteering. An island of course has a much longer coastline than a corresponding area of the mainland, while the interior lines make every part much more accessible. We no longer move in an area where the alien sea meets our familiar earth habitat and from which we can retreat at will, but are cut off instead by the encircling sea which must be crossed in both advance and retreat.

As we move our viewpoint islands vary in contour and character in much the same way as do hills and mountains. They change these same attributes too as the tide rises and falls, pulsating in height and area in step with the sea. When we move our viewpoint in an archipelago, the continued coalescing and separating of the component islets make for further fascinating variety.

The major islands adjacent to the South West Peninsula Coast Path are Lundy, athwart the mouth of the Bristol Channel, and the bigger inhabited islands of the Scillonian archipelago. Numerous lesser islands close to the coastline have been mentioned in the text and some are listed below. There is no island included in the route of the Path and visits will always be diversions beside the way.

Lundy is 3 miles long by half a mile wide so that its 'coast path' has a length of some 7 miles. There is indeed path or open hillside all the way and the going is very comparable with the mainland, say in the south part of West Penwith, where the granite cliffs give very similar background scenery. Unfortunately this walk cannot be accomplished within the day tripper's time limit, the White Funnel Steamer service from Ilfracombe providing only about 2½hr on shore. The traveller who stays on the island (hotel; cottages by previous arrangement; camping with previous permission) comes more probably on the tender from Bideford. He will be amply rewarded by as fine a cliff top walk as can be found anywhere, passing en route the Shutter Rock and the Devil's Limekiln, various rock pinnacles (the Needle, the Devil's Chimney and the Constable), the Earthquake, the Devil's Slide, Rat and Mouse Islands, Marisco Castle, the Old Battery and the Brazen Ward. There are some caves and some rock climbs, two lighthouses and a church and a public house with elastic opening hours. Lundy was acquired only recently by the National Trust and one would like to feel that its own special character will be preserved indefinitely thereby.

St Mary's, with the attached mass of the Hugh, the largest of the Scillies, has a coastal perimeter of 8½ miles. Anyone wishing to see as many as possible of the other islands must stay here (hotels; general accommodation; camp sites) to take advantage of the efficient boat services which leave the harbour every morning and afternoon, returning in the evening in time for dinner. These day trips give the visitor up to six hours on each of the other inhabited islands and access to the following coastal walks: St Agnes and the Gugh (5 miles), which are linked by a sandbank covered at high tide; St Martin's and White Island (7 miles), linked by a shingle bank covered at high tide; Tresco (5½ miles) with its famous gardens and a cave called Piper's Hole, elusive but deep if you can find it; Bryher (4½ miles). These islands are truly delightful, but nowadays very large numbers of people know it. St Mary's is crowded in the season, while the other islands have comparatively large numbers of visitors on every fine day. It is not possible to walk very far without meeting fellow explorers so that nowhere is there a real feeling of remoteness. Camping on the off-islands is probably the answer—it is allowed by previous arrangement on St Agnes and St Martin's; there is a little holiday accommodation also. Either would be beautifully quiet in the evening. A private boat to visit the smaller islands would also open up the possibilities. Wild life is abundant, antiquities abound; there are sea caves and a little rock climbing. Access is by steamer or helicopter from Penzance.

Of the other West Country islands, St Michael's Mount in Mounts Bay, a foreshore island, has a castle and a small village; Burgh Island in Bigbury Bay has an hotel and Drake's Island in Plymouth Sound an Adventure Training Centre; Brownsea Island in Poole Harbour is a nature sanctuary. Islands which have been inhabited at some time include St Helen's, Tean, Samson and Great Arthur in the Scillies, the Mew Stone off Wembury and Looe Island. Lesser islands, stacks and pinnacles are legion. Some, like Enys Dodnan at Land's End, as easily accessible; some, like Black-church Rock at Mouth Mill, are straightforward climbing prob-lems; some need the most advanced techniques of coasteering in the surmounting, for example Bear Rock at Hartland Quay; some remain unclimbed—the Steeple by Bolt Tail, some of the fearsome sandstone pinnacles at Ladram Bay and at Dawlish, and so on. Sometimes a boat may be needed for access, though there may not be any particular climbing problem at the far side—many of the lesser rocks of Scilly come within this category, as do a host of others nearer the mainland.

Islands have a special appeal for the traveller, particularly if he be mountaineer also, and it is well worth while to turn aside occasionally to tackle the problems of access presented by the wide assortment of islands which lines our route.

Bibliography

Borlase, W., *The Islands of Scilly*, 1756. Reprint, Newcastle, 1966
Etherton, P. T. and Barlow, V., *Lundy–The Tempestuous Isle*, 1960
Gade, F. W., *Lundy–Bristol Channel*, n.d.
Kay, E., *Isles of Flowers*, 1963
Langham, M. and A., *Lundy*, Newton Abbot, 1970
Mumford, L., *Portrait of the Isles of Scilly*, 1968
Vyvyan, C. C., *The Scilly Isles*, 1960

IX

SHIPPING AND COASTLINES

AT the sea's edge the relation between the distance of the visible horizon (d miles) and the height of the eye of the observer (h feet) is given by the empirical formula $d = 1·3\sqrt{h}$ (ie on the beach d is $3\frac{1}{4}$ miles; on a 400ft cliff it is 26 miles). An object beyond this distance will start to be cut off by the curvature of the earth. To decide whether two objects are intervisible we work out the distance of the visible horizon from each; if these two distances added together are less than the actual distance, then one cannot be seen from the other. Thus Lundy 466ft (d = 28 miles) and Trevose Head 243ft (d = 20 miles), which are 47 miles apart, are just intervisible, while Lizard 250ft (d = 21 miles) and Rame Head 380ft (d = $25\frac{1}{2}$ miles), which are 50 miles apart, are not.

Much of the way the walker on the Path looks down on passing shipping as with the eye of a bird. Everywhere he will see tiny boats going about their local business—fishing, pleasure trips, and so forth. Indeed at almost any point he can charter a boat and be taken for a new look at the cliffs and the caves, pinnacles, and arches. But the places to see large ocean-going passenger and cargo ships, and sometimes even warships, are the big promontories, like the Lizard, which jut out far enough to deflect the sea lanes. The uninstructed observer will only be able to identify the main groups of ships—merchant ships, warships, fishing vessels, pleasure craft, sailing vessels, harbour craft etc, though he may perhaps recognise some types within the groups and be able to distinguish a tanker from a cargo ship, a cruiser from a destroyer and so on. The game becomes much more interesting with the aid of silhouettes (see Bibliography, the first two items); unfortunately there is no room to print a selection here: eventually developing knowledge can embrace national characteristics of design, hull colours, house flags, etc.

The Path passes three major ports: Falmouth (cargo), Plymouth (cargo and naval), and Portland (naval). Here a selection of the largest vessels is always available for distant study. In the many smaller places the vessels too are smaller, but we have the advantage of seeing them closer at hand. Apart from very large numbers of pleasure trips in the summer months scheduled steamer services run along the North Devon coast, from Penzance to St Mary's and from Weymouth to the Channel Isles.

Along the cliff top we come across a range of aids and signals to travellers upon the ocean. Most spectacular are the lighthouses, which by their prominent siting and distinctive beam patterns guide the mariner safely along our shores by day and by night. Four West Country lights are sea-based—Longships, Bishop, Wolf, and Eddystone; the remainder, which are served from the shore, are usually on show to visitors during summer months (except at times when the fog signals are sounding). The most modern trend is indicated by three which are fully automatic—Peninnis Head, Tater Dû, and Godrevy Island. Closely akin are the lightships—the Seven Stones, above the site of Lyonnesse, and the Shambles off Portland; here the tendency is to replace them where possible by fully automatic light buoys, one of which will take the place of Shambles in the near future. Smaller sea hazards are marked by whistling, or moaning or bell buoys which, as at Runnel Stone, Udder Rock, etc, warn by their distinctive sounds. All these fall in the charge of Trinity House, whose West Country depot is at Penzance.

To help to fix his position, the daytime navigator uses sightings and alignments on prominent buildings, church towers, pillars, etc, on the shore—collectively known as daymarks. We pass many of them on our cliff-top way—Rame Head, St Aldhelm's Head, St Keverne Church, Gribbin Head, Stepper Point, and so on. Sometimes a pair of such beacons is lined on an offshore feature, for example those at Porthgwarra which point to the Runnel Stone.

In addition to the buoys marking sea hazards, a range of shapes and colours is used to indicate the navigable channel in an estuary. There are three main shapes: conical (black, or black and white) marking the right hand side of the channel when entering from the sea; flat-topped (red, or red and white) marking the left hand side; spherical (banded red and white) marking sandbanks or shoals in mid-channel. Wreck buoys are green with white lettering; many others smaller are used for a variety of purposes—mooring, marking nets and lobster pots, etc.

Judging from the extensive literature one might expect to find wrecks all over the place. In fact they are rare. Many of the life-boats which deal so competently with such emergencies are open for inspection by the passing traveller. Sometimes we may see salvage in progress and can marvel at the feats of engineering carried out with somewhat rusty and dilapidated-looking equipment by salvagers working from the cliff top.

At lighthouses and at coastguard stations storm cones are exhibited as a warning to mariners when a gale is expected within twelve hours. A cone three feet high is hoisted on a mast, point up for a northerly gale and down for a southerly. When the cones are out even the traveller on the cliff path must look out for himself. During a big storm, when water whipped from the surface of the sea is blown horizontally along the cliff tops or when huge waves striking the cliff base can splash up to three hundred feet or more, the cliff edge should be left to the elements.

On the cliff tops we often come across strongly constructed look-out posts having large areas of window commanding the sea. Some are Lloyds' Signal Stations, where the shipping intelligence of the nation is compiled from observation and exchange of signals with passing ships. The remainder belong to HM Coastguard, which is a part of the Board of Trade. Long ago this organisation dealt with smuggling by constant patrolling of the cliffs and many of today's cliff top routes take the lines of the original coastguard paths. To fulfil this role the manpower was widespread and we still find characteristic coastguard houses in most seaside places. Now the Service is more concentrated and its function is largely sea safety and rescue.

Walkers on the Path will be able to carry out a detailed surveillance of the coast very much as did the old coastguards, and in emergency they may still be able to play a real part by alerting the modern coastguard rescue organisation. If therefore you see any of the following distress signals out to sea, dial 999 at the earliest opportunity and inform the coastguard:

(a) Rocket parachute flare or hand flare (showing red light)
(b) Rockets or shells throwing red stars one at a time at short intervals
(c) Smoke signals with orange-coloured smoke
(d) Any signalling method reproducing the morse letters SOS ($- - - \cdot \cdot \cdot - - -$) or the word 'Mayday'

(e) Figure slowly and repeatedly raising and lowering outstretched arms

(f) Continuous sounding of any fog-signalling apparatus

(g) Flames on a vessel from a burning tar barrel

(h) International code signal of distress NC (blue and white chequered flag with 16 squares above a flag striped horizontally blue, white, red, white, blue

(i) A square flag with a ball below it

(j) Red ensign upside down

(k) Red ensign made fast high in the rigging

(l) Coat or article of clothing on an oar (small boats)

Look specially for distress signals from large ships offshore, or close inshore, which are stationary or listing, and from vessels of any size on fire. There is obvious emergency when small boats are seen to have capsized, aeroplanes land in the sea, airmen are seen dropping by parachute or when people are seen in the water. A coloured poster No. CG 22, which sets out the whole of the above, is displayed prominently all along the coastline.

Bibliography

Dodman, F. E., *The Observer's Book of Ships*, 1966
Hampton, T. A., *The Sailor's World*, Newton Abbot, 1968
Nos. 14, 17, 18, 19, 30, 33, 34, and 50 from the General Bibliography

X

A NOTE ON THE WEATHER

CONSTANT weather forecasts stream across the ether and are heard as a matter of course by a high proportion of the population. The traveller can always find out by asking, if indeed he is not already carrying a portable radio for this and other purposes. The Shipping Forecasts, which are the most detailed, divide the British seas into areas—those of immediate interest are Lundy (Minehead to Land's End), Plymouth (Land's End to Start Point) and Portland (Start Point to Bournemouth Bay). Those from which the weather will most likely be coming are Finisterre, Sole, Fastnet, and Shannon.

The jargon for visibility used in the forecasts is related to distance as follows:

0 Dense Fog (50yd), 1 Thick Fog (1/10 miles), 2 Fog (1/5 miles), 3 Moderate Fog ($\frac{1}{2}$ mile), 4 Very Poor Visibility (1 mile), 5 Poor Visibility (2 miles), 6 Moderate Visibility (5 miles), 7 Good Visibility (10 miles), 8 Very Good Visibility (30 miles), 9 Excellent Visibility (above 30 miles).

Unfortunately good visibility is usually associated with incipient bad weather.

A useful weather rule, described in detail in the reference, is the so-called crossed-winds rule. Stand with your back to the lower winds, or the direction of motion of the lower clouds, then if the upper winds or clouds come from the left the weather will deteriorate, if from the right it will improve, if parallel then no marked change is likely.

Bibliography

Watts, A., *Instant Weather Forecasting*, 1968

XI

THE PRESENT STATE OF THE PATH

1 *Minehead–Lynton.* The status of the path from Old Barrow Hill to behind Foreland Point is obscure.

2 *Lynton–Lee Bay.* At present Sherrycombe must be missed by a detour on minor roads and Great Hangman cannot be traversed. Between Water Mouth and Hele the line is obscure; the path is poor and the road gives better going.

3 *Lee Bay–Peppercombe.* The line is difficult to follow from Braunton Burrows into Braunton.

4 *Peppercombe–Combe Valley.* Lines are obscure and paths overgrown on either side of Buck's Mills, Clovelly to Mouth Mill is permissive only. There is no path between Mouth Mill and Shipload Bay and lanes inland have to be followed.

5 *Combe Valley–Tintagel.* One or two places are overgrown between Millook Haven and Crackington Haven.

6 *Tintagel–Trevose Head.* The route between Trebarwith Strand and Port Gaverne is little used. There is no route at the sea's edge between Pinehaven and Portquin—the direct path is imperative.

7 *Trevose Head–Perranporth.* The inland route round the range at Holywell is imperative.

8 *Perranporth–St Ives.* The cliff edge route past Nancekuke is normally open—only occasionally closed. Hayle Ferry is irregular.

9 *St Ives–Land's End.* The field path is recommended at present from St Ives to Gurnard's Head. The cliff path is overgrown all the way to Portheras.

10 *Land's End–Trewavas Head.* Penberth to Tater Dû is overgrown and there are breaks. Lamorna to Mousehole must be taken by the inland path at present.

11 *Trewavas Head–Black Head.* Trewavas Head to Porthleven is overgrown in places.

12 *Black Head–Nare Head.* From St Anthony to Helford road and footpath inland have to be used at present. The path below Mawnan is permissive only. The ferry from St Mawes to Place is doubtful.

13 *Nare Head–Fowey*. Caerhayes to Hemmick Beach must be taken on the road by Boswinger. There is no path yet between Pentewan and Porthpean. From Par Sands to Polkerris there is a path but no right of way.

14 *Fowey–Portwrinkle*. From Lantic Bay to Polperro there is no path except for the last mile—roads etc inland must be used. Between Millendreath and Seaton and between Beacon and Portwrinkle there is no path as yet and inland roads must be used.

15 *Portwrinkle–St Anchorite's Rock*. The path round Mount Edgcumbe is not available. There is no path from Beacon Hill to St Anchorite's Rock.

16 *St Anchorite's Rock–Slapton*. No path from St Anchorite's Rock to Mothecombe. The ferry at Bantham is doubtful.

17 *Slapton–Watcombe Head*. There is no path yet between Kingswear and Scabbacombe.

18 *Watcombe Head–Ladram Bay*.

19 *Ladram Bay–Lyme Regis*.

20 *Lyme Regis–Abbotsbury*.

21 *Abbotsbury–Durdle Door*.

22 *Durdle Door–South Haven Point*.

Note: Places which are overgrown are likely to be cleared in the near future; places where the line is obscure will be waymarked and signposted. Local enquiries should be made.

GENERAL BIBLIOGRAPHY

1 Anon., *Guide to all the Watering and Sea Bathing Places*, 1820
2 Arber, E. A. N., *The Coast Scenery of North Devon*, 1911
3 Baddeley, M. J. B. and Ward, C. S., *Thorough Guide–North Devon and North Cornwall*, 1908
4 ——— *Thorough Guide–South Devon and South Cornwall*, 1903
5 Betjeman, J., *Cornwall (Shell Guide)*, 1964
6 *Black's Guide–Cornwall*, numerous editions
7 *Black's Guide–Devon*, numerous editions
8 Boyle, V. C. and Payne, D., *Devon Harbours*, 1952
9 Burton, S. H., *The Coasts of Cornwall*, 1955
10 ——— *The North Devon Coast*, 1953
11 ——— *The South Devon Coast*, 1954
12 Camden, William, *Britannia*, 1586 in Latin; subsequent translations. Reprinted Newton Abbot, 1971
13 Carew, Richard, *The Survey of Cornwall*. Reprinted with John Norden's Maps, 1953
14 Carter, C., *Cornish Shipwrecks–The North Coast*, Newton Abbot, 1970
15 Duncan, R., *Devon and Cornwall*, 1966
16 Esquiros, A., *Cornwall and its Coasts*, 1865
17 Farr, G., *Wreck and Rescue on the Bristol Channel*, Truro, 1966
18 ——— *Wreck and Rescue on the Coast of Devon*, Truro, 1968
19 ——— *Wreck and Rescue on the Dorset Coast*, Truro, 1969
20 Folliott Stokes, A. G., *The Cornish Coast and Moors*, n.d.
21 Harper, C. G., *The Cornish Coast (North)*, 1910
22 ——— *The Cornish Coast (South)*, 1910
23 ——— *The Dorset Coast*, 1905
24 ——— *The North Devon Coast*, 1908
25 ——— *The Somerset Coast*, 1909
26 ——— *The South Devon Coast*, 1907
27 Heath, S., *The South Devon and Dorset Coast*, 1910
28 Hockin, J. R. A., *Walking in Cornwall*, 1944
29 Leland, John, *Itinerary 1534–43*. First published 1710, reprinted 1964
30 Larn, R. and Carter, C., *Cornish Shipwrecks–2 Volumes*, Newton Abbot, 1969–70
31 Manning Sanders, R., *The West of England*, 1949

32 Maton, W. G., *Observations on the Western Counties of England*, 1794–96
33 Noall, C., *Cornish Lights and Shipwrecks*, Truro, 1968
34 Noall, C. and Farr, G., *Wreck and Rescue on the Cornish Coast*, 3 volumes, Truro, 1966–69
35 Norden, John, *A Topographical and Historical Description of Cornwall, 1584*. First published 1728, reprinted 1966
36 Norway, A. H., *Highways and Byways in Devon and Cornwall*, 1897
37 Page, J. L. W., *The Coasts of Devon and Lundy Island*, 1895
38 Pridham, L., *The Dorset Coastline*, Dorchester, n.d.
39 Pyatt, E. C., *A Climber in the West Country*, Newton Abbot, 1968
40 *Red Guide, The Dorset Coast* (also bound carrying the additional title *Bridport/West Bay*, or *Lyme Regis*, or *Swanage*, or *Weymouth*)
41 ——— *North Cornwall* (also bound carrying the additional titles *Bude*, or *Newquay*)
42 ——— *North West Devon* (also bound carrying the additional titles *Barnstaple*, or *Bideford*, or *Ilfracombe*)
43 ——— *South Cornwall* (also bound carrying the additional titles *Falmouth*, or *Fowey*, or *Looe*)
44 ——— *South Devon* (also bound carrying the additional titles *Dartmouth*, or *Paignton*, or *Salcombe/Kingsbridge*, or *Torquay*)
45 ——— *South East Devon* (also bound carrying the additional titles *Budleigh Salterton*, or *Dawlish*, or *Exeter*, or *Exmouth*, or *Sidmouth*, or *Teignmouth*)
46 ——— *West Cornwall* (also bound carrying the additional titles *Penzance*, or *St Ives*)
47 Roddis, R., *Cornish Harbours*, 1951
48 Salmon, A. L., *The Cornwall Coast*, 1912
49 Steers, J. A., *The Coastline of England and Wales*, 1947
50 Stoker, H., *The Seaside Pocket Companion*, 1956 (republished as the *Arrow Seaside Companion*, 1966)
51 Treves, F., *Highways and Byways in Dorset*, 1906
52 Watson, B., *Devon (Shell Guide)*, 1964
53 White, W., *A Londoner's Walk to the Land's End*, 1879

ACKNOWLEDGEMENTS

I should like to thank the following for help in various ways: Keith Lawder, for the part he played in the original inspiration and for contributing an appendix; Cyril Manning, for other appendices Messrs T. G. Millar, S. P. Taylor and R. F. Brown of the Country-side Commission for copious information and for helpful criticism The County Planning Officer for Cornwall and Mr H. Green; The County Surveyor for Devon and Mr D. White; The County Surveyor for Dorset and Mr C. Rushen; The County Librarians of Cornwall Devon and Dorset; The Libraries of the Alpine Club and of the Borough of Richmond upon Thames; Aerofilms Ltd for all photographic illustrations, The Staff of Aerofilms Library, London; Peter Simple and the *Daily Telegraph*, for permission to quote; The Information Division of the Board of Trade; The Ordnance Survey, for data on which maps were based; Edward Zenthon and Jaqui Nudds, for map production; Ian Boyes and Edward and Diana Bullock.

Marguerite, Christopher and Gillian Pyatt have given support, encouragement and practical help at all stages.

Edward C. Pyatt

Hampton, September, 1970.